FORMAN'S

Guide To Third Reich German Awards...And Their Values

1st EDITION

I wish to dedicate this book to

Dr. KURT G. KLIETMANN

Direktor der Instituts für wissenschaftliche Ordenskunde
Berlin, W. Germany

In grateful thanks for his generosity and help in sup-
plying the great majority of the photographs used in
this catalogue which form part of the photographic
library of the Instituts für wissenschaftliche Ordenskunde and for his kindness to the Forman family
over many years.

The front and back cover photographs are of a unique German Arts and Science award, circa 1938. This massive, handcrafted piece is of gold-plated silver and is constructed of twenty separate pieces. It is probable that it is a Grade of Office of the Order, e.g., Secretary of the Order and President of the Order.

1st Edition

Published by Adrian Forman, 13 Shepherd Market, Mayfair, London W1Y 7HR, England

INTRODUCTION

I would like to introduce you to the invaluable English language international price-guide catalogue for Third Reich Decorations, Medals, Badges & Awards 1933-1945. As you may know, there have been several German [national] price-guide catalogues which have been of some guidance to German collectors. However, these have been mainly on Imperial German awards, with the Third Reich section in the back. The prices have been merely a guide, without taking into account the considerable difference in quality and value of such items as early and late war manufactured awards. In addition, the producers of these catalogues [with the exception of Lothar Hartung] were not specialists on the Third Reich period awards and did not do justice to the value of the rarer and less attainable pieces. However, at the time, these catalogues did fill the gap on the subject. I intend not only to fill the gap but to give you a work that satisfies your need for a comprehensive publication on values and identification of Third Reich awards. On the subject of values, presentation documents & certificates when awarded to famous personalities become far more valuable than the basic prices shown, unless they are extremely rare anyway. The basic prices reflected in my book have been derived from reviewing the results of annual international auctions and then establishing an average price range for each piece. This does include the document, the award container and in some cases, the cloth version. When an asterisk has been used, it denotes "one of a kind" or an extremely rare item upon which a value cannot be determined.

As this catalogue is the first of its kind for worldwide collectors, it reflects the prices in the international market of the United States and Europe. I considered such an undertaking several years ago, when in the midst of producing the "Forman Special Colour Catalogues." I felt very strongly that there was a necessity for an international standard price-guide catalogue (Illustrated) as used by both Seaby's (of London) 3 and later Spinks (of London) with their respective coin & medal price catalogues. These became standard books of reference in regard to prices (worldwide) to collectors, dealers, investors, auctioneers and others.

Since conceiving the idea some seven years ago there has been a substantial increase in the worldwide market for Third Reich awards & militaria. Most recently, Germany has become second only to the United States in growth, both in increased public interest and in price increases, particularly at leading auction halls. Great Britain has now taken third place in growth and general interest, although there is an excellent collecting fraternity and there are several well-known authors (the 1968 Littlejohn & Dodkins book by R.J. Bender of the United States was the first of its kind). The hobby has great potential for future growth!

In more than twenty years I have seen this hobby grow to become even more internationally collected than antique arms, armour, antique guns, British medals or French Napoleonic militaria. This is a most impressive record regardless of the better copies, fakes or reproductions that have appeared on the market.

Although in some cases certain awards can increase in value every year, the German promotional idea of new additions annually with few, if any, genuine price increases is merely a way of selling more books. In reality, a new price guide is only required every two years. Thus, a revised edition with new prices will be available in 1990/91.

Finally, my advice to all collectors is to buy from known, reputable sources, where stock is guaranteed and backed by the knowledge that makes such guarantees valid. Purchase good reference books, some of which are listed in this work. Whenever possible, view collections and handle the items. There is no substitute for experience, combined with a good basic understanding of your subject.

ADRIAN FORMAN

13 Shepherd Market
Mayfair
London W1Y 7HR
England
Tel: (01): 629-6599

NOTE:

The price of certificates can vary greatly from the values listed in this book. These variances are based on the recipient of the document (i.e., a prominent figure, Knight's Cross holder, general, etc.) and the signer.

ACKNOWLEDGEMENTS

Individuals:

J.R. Angolia
Wm. Chizar
G. Del Collo
Stan Cook
Don Frailey
David Fuller
Roger Hall
Jeff Hanson
Bud Hasher

Tom Jayne
Bob Kraus
Ken Lazier
David Littlejohn
Dr. Neumann
George Petersen
Jost W. Schneider
Bob Seitz
Tom Shutt

Andy Southard
Otto Spronk
Joe Stone
Bill Stump
Jerry Weiblen
H. Winch
Steve Wolfe

Institutions:

Mohawk Arms
National Archives
West Point Museum Collection

The author, Adrian Forman, has dealt with and collected medals for over twenty years. As an internationally recognized expert on this subject, he has been consulted by both Sotheby's and Christie's of London for his opinions on orders and medals. He has also contributed, for some years, to several of R. James Bender Publishing's (USA) specialized books on 3rd Reich subjects.

1. **Spanish Cross in Gold with Swords & Diamonds**
   (Spanienkreuz--mit Schwertern in Gold und Brillanten)
   (a) Type A Award issue, hallmarked silver, diamonds $12,500
   (b) Type B Private Jewellers copy dress piece (sapphires) 7,500
   (c)   Certificate 5,000
   (d)   Case 350

Nr. 1

Adolf Galland wearing the Spanish Cross in Gold with Swords and Diamonds.

2. Spanish Cross in Gold with Swords
(mit Schwertern)

(a)	Type A Deluxe hallmarked silver/gilt	**$950**
(b)	Type B Gilt bronze issue	650
(c)	Certificate	750
(d)	Case	150

3. Spanish Cross in Silver with Swords
(mit Schwertern)

(a)	Type A Early hallmarked silver, fine quality	$600
(b)	Type B Later type silver-plated	400
(c)	Certificate	500
(d)	Case	150

Nr's. 2, 3 & 5

George Petersen

Nr's. 4 & 6

4. Spanish Cross in Silver without Swords
(ohne Schwerter)

(a)	Type A. Early hallmarked silver, fine quality	$850
(b)	Type B. Later type silver-plated	550
(c)	Certificate	750
(d)	Case	150

5. Spanish Cross in Bronze with Swords
(mit Schwerter)

(a)	Type A Bronze, early deluxe type with cutout Swastika detail	$450
(b)	Type B Bronze, solid Swastika detail	400
(c)	Certificate	400
(d)	Case	150

Im Namen
des
Deutschen Volkes
verleihe ich

dem Leutnant
Wilhelm Boddem

in Anerkennung
seiner ganz hervorragenden Leistungen
als Freiwilliger im spanischen Freiheitskampf
das
Deutsche Spanien-Kreuz
in
Gold mit Schwertern und Brillanten

Berlin, den 6. Juni 1939
Der Führer
und
Oberste Befehlshaber
der Wehrmacht

Im Namen
des
Deutschen Volkes
verleihe ich

dem Unteroffizier Ernst B a r t z

in Anerkennung
seiner hervorragenden Leistungen
als Freiwilliger im spanischen Freiheitskampf
das
Deutsche Spanien-Kreuz
in
Gold mit Schwertern

Berlin, den 6. Juni 1939
Der Führer
und
Oberste Befehlshaber
der Wehrmacht

Im Namen
des
Deutschen Volkes
verleihe ich

dem Diplom-Ingenieur Joachim von   Richthofen

als Anerkennung
für seine Leistungen
im spanischen Freiheitskampf
das
Deutsche Spanien-Kreuz
in
Silber

Berlin, den 6.Juni 1939.
Der Führer
und
Oberste Befehlshaber
der Wehrmacht

Im Namen
des
Deutschen Volkes

verleihe ich

dem

Angestellten Wilhelm B o d d e m

und

seiner Ehefrau Barbara geb. Vitt

das Ehrenkreuz für hinterbliebene deutscher Spanienkämpfer

Berlin, den 17. Januar 1940

Der Führer
und
Oberste Befehlshaber
der Wehrmacht

Göring is shown presenting a Spanish Cross to Uffz. Kies on the morning of 4 June 1939 at Döberitz.

6. **Spanish Cross in Bronze without Swords**
   (ohne Schwerter)
   (a) Type A Bronze, early deluxe type with cutout Swastika detail $450
   (b) Type B Bronze, solid Swastika detail 400
   (c)   Certificate 400
   (d)   Case 150

7. **Cross of Honor for Relatives of the Dead in Spain (German)**
   (Ehrenkreuz für Hinterbliebene deutscher Spanienkämpfer)
   (a) Type A Bronze, olive brown color $1,000
   (b) Type B Hallmarked silver, bronze finish with maker's stamp 750
   (c)   Certificate 750
   (d)   Case 350

8. **Tank Badge of the Legion Condor**
   (Panzertruppen-Abzeichen der Legion Condor)
   (a) Type A First issue badge in solid silver $1,250
   (b) Type B Second issue in white metal 750
   (c)   Unique badge in solid gold awarded to Col. von Thoma .... *
   (d)   Certificate 1,500

9. **Commemorative Cloth Cuff Title "Spain 1936-39"**
   (Ärmelband "1936 SPANIEN 1939")
   (a) Type A Bevo flat silk (maroon) and gold wire, deluxe quality $750
   (b) Type B Cotton/bullion variations 500
   (c)   Certificate 500

The so-called "Spanish Wound Badge" is catalogued
with 1936-45 Wound Badges Section.

Nr. 7

George Petersen

Nr. 7(d)

George Petersen

Nr. 8

Uffz. Erwin Völker shortly before the Berlin victory parade on 6 June 1939.

Roger Hall

1936 Spanien 1939

Nr. 9(b)

13

ORDERS, DECORATIONS, AND MEDALS OF
THE ARMED FORCES 1939-45

10. Grand Cross of the Iron Cross 1939
(Eisernes Kreuz - Grosskreuz)

(a) Type A $12,000

> Cross awarded to Reichsmarschall Göring. Hallmarked '800' and marked "L/12" ("Juncker" of Berlin) - several specimens exist.

(b) Type B Crosses manufactured for museum and exhibition displays 3,000
(c) Large presentation illuminated vellum document in folder .... *
(d) Deluxe presentation red leather, large case 5,000

Nr. 10

11. **Knights Cross of the Iron Cross with Golden Oakleaves, Swords & Diamonds**
   (Ritterkreuz des E.K. mit dem Eichenlaub in Gold mit Schwertern und Brillanten)

(a) Type A Presented by Hitler to Rudel. In gold with diamonds-
   apparently two or three examples exist. . . . .   *
(b) Type B Unknown . . . .   *
(c)   Large presentation illuminated vellum document in folder . . .   *
(d)   Case . . . .   *

Hans-Ulrich Rudel.

Nr. 12

12. **Knights Cross of the Iron Cross with Oakleaves, Swords & Diamonds**
   (Ritterkreuz des E.K. mit dem Eichenlaub mit Schwertern und Brillanten)

(a) Type A Issue type in hallmarked silver studded with precious stones . . $15,000
(b) Type B Issue type in hallmarked platinum with precious stones   15,000
(c) Type C Jeweller's dress copy in hallmarked silver
            studded with semi-precious stones (variations)   7,500
(d)   Large presentation illuminated vellum document in folder . . .   20,000
(e)   Case   500   **15**

Nr. 13(c)

13. Knights Cross of the Iron Cross with Oakleaves & Swords (Ritterkreuz mit dem Eichenlaub und Schwertern

(a) Type A Issue type in hallmarked "800" silver.
Reverse of swords plain (flat). 2,000-5,000

(b) Type B Deluxe private purchase type, hallmarked silver
and maker's mark. Reverse of swords detailed.   7,500

(c)   Large presentation illuminated vellum document in folder   20,000

(d)   Case   300

Nr. 13

Nr. 14

George Petersen

14. Knights Cross of the Iron Cross with Oakleaves (Ritterkreuz mit dem Eichenlaub)

16 (a) Type A Issue type in hallmarked silver & maker's mark $4,000

(b)	Type B	Jeweller's dress copy, hallmarked silver & maker's mark.	
		Late war examples with silver-plated finish only	2,000-3,000
(c)		Preliminary certificate	2,500
(d)		Large presentation illuminated vellum document in white leather folder; usually signed by Hitler	10,000
(e)		Case	300

Nr. 14(d)

IM NAMEN
DES DEUTSCHEN VOLKES
VERLEIHE ICH
DEM ℠-OBERGRUPPENFÜHRER
JOSEF DIETRICH
DAS EICHENLAUB
ZUM RITTERKREUZ
DES EISERNEN KREUZES

FÜHRERHAUPTQUARTIER
DEN 3. DEZEMBER 1941

DER FÜHRER
UND OBERSTE BEFEHLSHABER
DER WEHRMACHT

Josef (Sepp) Dietrich's vellum document for the Oak Leaves to his Knights Cross.

15. Knights Cross of the Iron Cross 1939 (Ritterkreuz des Eisernen Kreuzes)

(a)	Type A	Issue type in hallmarked silver some with maker's mark	$2,000
(b)	Type B	Jeweller's Dress copy, hallmarked silver, some with maker's marks. Late war examples exist with non-iron centers and silver-plated finish only	1,000-1,500
(c)		Preliminary certificate	1,000
(d)		Large presentation illuminated vellum document in red leather folder; usually signed by Hitler	3,000
(e)		Case	300

17

Nr. 15

IM NAMEN
DES DEUTSCHEN VOLKES
VERLEIHE ICH
DEM OBERSTLEUTNANT I.G.
TORSTEN CHRIST
DAS RITTERKREUZ
DES EISERNEN KREUZES

FÜHRERHAUPTQUARTIER
DEN 24. OKTOBER 1942

DER FÜHRER
UND OBERSTE BEFEHLSHABER
DER WEHRMACHT

Nr. 15(d)

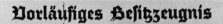

Vorläufiges Besitzeugnis

Der Führer
und Oberste Befehlshaber
der Wehrmacht

hat

dem Kapitänleutnant Karl-Heinz Moehle

das Ritterkreuz
des Eisernen Kreuzes

am 26.Februar 1941 verliehen.

Berlin , den 14. März 1941.

Kapitän zur See und Abt.Chef im MPA.

D. Frailey

Nr. 15(c)

16. **Iron Cross 1st Class 1939**
   (Eisernes Kreuz 1 Klasse)

(a)	Type A	Early quality award or screwback type	$75-95
(b)	Type B	Late war type	50
(c)		Certificate	100
(d)		Case	25

Nr. 16

Im Namen des führers
und Obersten Befehlshabers
der Wehrmacht

verleihe ich

dem

Gefreiten

Herbert F l e i s c h e r

II./K.G. 53

das

Eiserne Kreuz 1. Klasse.

Stabsquartier ....,den 20. Dezember 1940.

Der Chef der Luftflotte 2
und Befehlshaber Nordwest

Göring

Generalfeldmarschall .
(Dienstgrad und Dienststellung)

Mohawk Arms

Nr. 16(c)

---

17. Bar to the Iron Cross 1st Class 1939
(Spange 1939 zum E.K. 1 Klasse 1914)

(a)	Type A	Early quality award, silver-plated	$95
(b)	Type B	Late war type, needle pin	60
(c)	Type C	Screwback type	125
(d)		Certificate	125
(e)		Case	50

Im Namen des führers
und Obersten Befehlshabers
der Wehrmacht

verleihe ich

dem

Oberstleutnant i. Genst.

Herbert R i e c k h o f f

die Spange zum
Eisernen Kreuz 1. Klasse.

Hauptquartier. d. Ob. d. L., den 20. Mai........ 1940.

Der Reichsminister der Luftfahrt
und Oberbefehlshaber der Luftwaffe

Generalfeldmarschall
(Dienstgrad und Dienststellung)

George Petersen

Nr. 17

Nr. 17(d)

20

Generalmajor Hans Schmidt wears the Bar to the Iron Cross 1st Class (Nr. 17). Note positioning of his other decorations.

Spange
zum
Eisernen Kreuz
1. Klasse

Nur vom Beliehenen zu öffnen

Cardboard container for the Bar to the Iron Cross 1st Class.

Preparations for award ceremonies of the Knight's Cross, German Cross, Iron Cross 1st and 2nd Class and War Merit Cross 1st and 2nd Class.

Note the manner of wear of the Bar to the Iron Cross 1st (Nr. 17) and 2nd Classes (Nr. 19) as worn by Generalleutnant von Schell.

18. Iron Cross 2nd Class 1939
(Eisernes Kreuz II Klasse)

(a)	Type A	Early quality award	$30-40
(b)	Type B	Late war type	20-30
(c)		Certificate	30-60
(d)		Titled paper packed or LDO case	20

Nr. 18

Mohawk Arms

✠

Im Namen des Führers
und Obersten Befehlshabers
der Wehrmacht

verleihe ich

dem

Gefreiten
Herbert Fleischer

5./K.G.53

das

Eiserne Kreuz 2.Klasse.

Gefechtstand ,den 30.Oktober 1940.

Der Kommandierende General
des II. Flieger - Korps

General der Flieger
(Dienstgrad und Dienststellung)

Nr. 18(c)

19. Bar to the Iron Cross 2nd Class 1939
(Spange 1939 zum E.K. II Klasse 1914)

(a)	Type A	Early quality award, silver-plated	$60
(b)	Type B	Late war type in war metal	45
(c)		Certificate	100
(d)		Titled paper packet	25

Nr. 19

23

Im Namen des Führers
und Obersten Befehlshabers
der Wehrmacht

verleihe ich

dem

Oberstleutnant i. Genst.

Herbert R i e c k h o f f

die Spange zum
Eisernen Kreuz 2. Klasse.

z.Zt. Stabsquartier ,den 10. April 19 40 .

Der Chef der Luftflotte 2
und Befehlshaber Nord

(Dienstgrad und Dienststellung)

General der Flieger

Nr. 19(c)

---

20. Roll of Honor Clasp for the Army 1941
(Ehrenblattspange - Heer)
(a)	**	Awarded to recipient mounted on Iron Cross ribbon	$750
(b)		Certificate	1,000
(c)		Case	150-200

21. Roll of Honor Clasp for the Navy 1943
(Ehrentafelspange - Kriegsmarine)
(a)	**	Awarded to recipient mounted on Iron Cross ribbon	$1,500
(b)		Certificate	1,200
(c)		Case	150-200

22. Roll of Honor Clasp for the Luftwaffe
(Ehrentafelspange - Luftwaffe)
(a)	**	Awarded to recipient mounted on Iron Cross ribbon	900
(b)		Certificate	1,000
(c)		Case	150-200

Nr. 20

Nr. 21   Nr. 22

Generalleutnant Wilhelm Heun wears the Army Roll of Honor Clasp.

23. **German Cross in Gold 1941**
   (Deutsches Kreuz)

(a)	Type A	Metal and enamel (4) or (6) rivets, some with maker's marks	$600-750
(b)	Type B	Bullion and cloth field service issue (green and blue-grey)*	125-150
(c)		Preliminary certificate	250
(d)		Large presentation certificate	400
(e)		Large case for Type A	100-150

Nr's. 23(a) & 24(a)

*on white $400
 on black 175

Nr's. 23(b) & 24(b)

25

24. German Cross in Silver 1941
(Deutsches Kreuz)

(a)	Type A	Metal and enamel (4) or (6) rivets some with maker's marks	$800
(b)	Type B	Bullion and cloth field service issue	350
(c)		Preliminary certificate	300
(d)		Large presentation certificate	450
(e)		Large case for Type A	100-150

25. Special Grade of the German Cross in Gold with Diamonds
(Deutschen Kreuzes in Gold mit Brillanten)

** Approximately 20 specimens were manufactured by Rath of Munich in silver with precious stones. Examples are known of large presentation red leather cases embossed on lid with National Emblem. $20,000

Nr. 25

26. Knight Cross of the War Merit Cross in Gold with Swords 1944
(Goldenes Ritterkreuz des KVK mit Schwertern)

(a)	Fine quality gold-plated silver	$5,000
(b)	Large presentation certificate	10,000
(c)	Large case	500

27. Knights Cross of the War Merit Cross in Gold without Swords 1944
(Goldenes Ritterkreuz des KVK ohne Schwerter)

(a)	Fine quality gold-plated silver	$5,000
(b)	Large presentation certificate	10,000
(c)	Large case	500

28. Knights Cross of the War Merit Cross with Swords 1940
(Ritterkreuz des KVK mit Schwertern)

(a)	Type A	Early issue type, quality hallmarked silver with maker's mark	$3,000
(b)	Type B	Late war issue, silver-plated	1,250
(c)		Large presentation certificate	7,500
(d)		Large blue case	300

Nr's. 26 & 28   Reverse of Nr's 26 & 28

Nr's. 27 & 29

**29. Knights Cross of the War Merit Cross without Swords 1940
(Ritterkreuz des KVK ohne Schwerter)**

(a)	Type A	Early issue type, quality hallmarked silver with maker's mark	$3,000
(b)	Type B	Late war issue, silver-plated	1,250
(c)		Large presentation certificate	7,500
(d)		Large blue case	300

VORLÄUFIGES BESITZZEUGNIS

IM NAMEN
DES DEUTSCHEN VOLKES

HABE ICH

DEM

ᛋᛋ-Standartenführer

Walter E w e r t

DAS RITTERKREUZ
DES KRIEGSVERDIENSTKREUZES
MIT SCHWERTERN

VERLIEHEN.

DIE BESITZURKUNDE FOLGT NACH.

Führer-Hauptquartier, den 26.Dezember 1944

DER FÜHRER

Nr. 28(c) (preliminary)

30. War Merit Cross, 1st Class with Swords 1939
(Kriegsverdienstkreuz mit Schwertern)

(a)	Type A	Early issue, quality silver-plated	$60
(b)	Type B	Late war issue, silvered metal	45
(c)		Certificate	60
(d)		Case	25

Nr. 30   Nr. 31

George Petersen

Jm Namen des Führers
und Oberſten Befehlshabers
der Wehrmacht
verleihe ich
dem

Oberstleutnant

Friedrich Grossenbräucker

Kdo.Fl.H.Bereich 6/XVII Agram

das

Kriegsverdienſtkreuz 1. Klaſſe
mit Schwertern

Gefechtsstand , den 30.Januar 1945
Der Oberbefehlshaber der
Luftflotte 4

Generaloberst.
(Dienſtgrad und Dienſtſtellung)

Nr. 30(c)

31. War Merit Cross, 1st Class Without Swords 1939
(Kriegsverdienstkreuz ohne Schwerter)

(a)	Type A	Early issue, quality silver-plated	$45
(b)	Type B	Late war issue, silvered metal	30
(c)		Certificate	50
(d)		Case	25

32. War Merit Cross, 2nd Class with Swords 1939
(Kriegsverdienstkreuz II mit Schwertern)

(a)	Type A Early issue type in bronze	$12-15
(b)	Type B Late war issue bronze metal or alloy	9-12
(c)	Certificate	25-35
(d)	Titled paper packet	10

33. War Merit Cross, 2nd Class without Swords 1939
(Kriegsverdienstkreuz II ohne Schwerter)

(a)	Type A Early issue type in bronze	$10-12
(b)	Type B Late war issue, bronze metal or alloy	8-10
(c)	Certificate	30
(d)	Titled paper packet	10

Nr. 32   Nr. 33

34. War Merit Medal 1939
(Kriegsverdienstmedaille)

(a)	** Struck in bronze	10-15
(b)	Certificate	35
(c)	Titled paper packet	10

Nr. 34   Nr. 34 (Reverse)

35. War Commemorative Medal 1939-1940
(Medaille zur Erinnerung an den Krieg 1939/1940)
**   Struck in iron but no awards made $250

Nr. 35

Reverse for
Nr's. 35 & 36

36. War Commemorative Medal 1939-1941
(Medaille zur Erinnerung an den Krieg 1939/1941)
**   Struck in iron but no awards made $250   31

37. **Commemorative Medal of 13 March 1938**
    (Medaille zur Erinnerung an den 13 März 1938)
    (a) **   Known as "Entry into Austria" medal,
                  silver-plated bronze $20-30
    (b)   Certificate 50-75
    (c)   Red case 25

38. **Commemorative Medal of 1 October 1938**
    (Medaille zur Erinnerung an den 1 Oktober 1938)
    (a) **   Known as "Entry into Sudetenland" medal in bronze $20-30
    (b)   Certificate 60
    (c)   Brown case 25

Nr's. 37, 38 & 40

Nr. 37

Nr. 38

George Petersen

Der führer und Reichskanzler

hat aus Anlaß der Wiedervereinigung
Österreichs mit dem Deutschen Reich

dem

            Gefreiten d.R.
            Ewald Hermet
            Knispel

die
**Medaille zur Erinnerung
an den 13. März 1938**
verliehen.

Berlin, den   22. Mai 1939

**Der Staatsminister
und Chef der Präsidialkanzlei
des führers und Reichskanzlers**

Meissner

Nr. 37(b)

39. **Prague Castle bar for Commemorative Medal of 1 October 1938**
    (Spange "Pragerburg")
(a) ** Struck in bronze, some with maker's mark $40
(b) Certificate 50-75
(c) Small LDO cartons or titled paper packets 15-20

Nr. 39

40. **Commemorative Medal of the Return of the Memel District 1939**
    (Medaille zur Erinnerung an die Heimkehr des Memellandes)
(a) Type A Early issue struck in bronze $135
(b) Type B Later issue in bronzed metal 120
(c) Certificate 100
(d) Red case 25

Nr. 40

Der führer und Reichskanzler

hat aus Anlaß der Wiedervereinigung des
Memellandes mit dem Deutschen Reich

SS-Gruppenführer
Karl Wolff
Berlin

die

Medaille zur Erinnerung
an die Heimkehr des Memellandes

verliehen.

Berlin, den 19. September 1939

Der Staatsminister
und Chef der Präsidialkanzlei
des führers und Reichskanzlers

Nr. 40(c)

41. West Wall Medal 1939
(Deutsches Schutzwall-Ehrenzeichen)

(a)	Type A	Early issue struck in bronze	$15
(b)	Type B	Later issue in bronzed metal or alloy	12
(c)		Certificate	50
(d)		Titled paper packet	10

Nr. 41   Nr. 41 (Reverse)

42. The Italo-German Campaign Medal in Africa 1941
(Medaille für den italienisch-deutschen Feldzug in Afrika)

(a)	Type A	Early issue struck in bronze with maker's mark	$50
(b)	Type B	Later issue in silvered or grey metal	30
(c)		Certificate	300
(d)		Titled cellophane packet	50

Awarded to both German and Italian Troops

Nr. 42

George Petersen

Nr. 42(c)

Nr. 42
(Reverse)

Besitzurkunde

Dem

Prüfmeister
Alfred A d e

wurde die

Erinnerungsmedaille
für den
italienisch-deutschen
Feldzug in Afrika
verliehen

Afrika, den 9. Juni 1942

III./Sturzkampfgeschwader 3

Unterschrift
H a u p t m a n n u.
Gruppenkommandeur.

43. Medal for the Winter Campaign in Russia 1941-1942
  (Medaille "Winterschlacht im Osten 1941-1942")
  (a) Type A Early issue with maker's mark $15-25
  (b) Type B Later issue in silvered or grey metal 20
  (c)   Certificate 25-50
  (d)   Titled paper packet 15

Nr. 43

Nr. 43
(Reverse)

George Petersen

IM NAMEN DES FÜHRERS
UND
OBERSTEN BEFEHLSHABERS
DER WEHRMACHT

IST DEM

Oberjäger Erwin F o r k e l

AM 15. Oktober 1942

DIE MEDAILLE
WINTERSCHLACHT IM OSTEN
1941/42
(OSTMEDAILLE)

VERLIEHEN WORDEN.

FÜR DIE RICHTIGKEIT:

H a u p t m a n n .

Nr. 43(c)

44. Bravery and Commemorative Medal of the Spanish "Blue Division"1941
  (Tapferkeits-und Erinnerungsmedaille der spanischen "Blauen Division")
  (a) Type A German manufacture, bronzed metal with maker's mark $45-60
  (b) Type B Spanish manufacture, poor quality 30
  (c)   Certificate 150
  (d)   Titled paper packet 30

Nr. 44

**Nr. 44
(Reverse)**

45. Spanish Decoration to Commemorate the Spanish "Blue Division" on The Russian Front 1941

(a) Type A   Fine quality silver-plated and enameled German manufacture   . $125

(b) Type B   Spanish manufacture, poorer quality and finish   75

Issued by General Franco

Nr's. 46(a) & (e)

36   **Nr. 45**

46. **Ostvolk Decorations for Bravery or Merit on the Eastern Front 1942**
(Tapferkeits-und Verdienst-Auszeichnung für Angehörige der Ostvölker)

(a)	1st Class in Gold with Swords	$75
(b)	2nd Class in Gold with Swords	45
(c)	1st Class in Gold	75
(d)	2nd Class in Gold	45
(e)	1st Class in Silver with Swords	55
(f)	2nd Class in Silver with Swords	45
(g)	1st Class in Silver	45-60
(h)	2nd Class in Silver	45
(i)	3rd Class in Bronze with Swords	45
(j)	3rd Class in Bronze	40
(k)	Certificate, bi-lingual in German and Russian	150-250
(l)	Black cases for 1st Class and Titled paper packets for 2nd and 3rd Class	30-50

Nr's. 46(c) & (g)

Nr's. 46(a), (c), (e) & (g) (Reverse)

Nr's. 46(b), (f) & (i)

Nr's. 46(d), (h) & (j)

47. **The Young Cossack Officer's School Badge c.1941**
   (Jung-Kosaken-Abzeichen)
   ** Reverse either pin-back or two loops $500
   Silvered metal. Hollow-back pressing.

Nr. 47

48. **5th Don Cossacks Cavalry Regiment Cross 1941**
   (5.Don Kosakenreiter-Rgt. Kreuz)
   ** Original issue matt colored paint on grey alloy
   with steel pin $750

49. **Cossacks Cross of the 2nd Siberian Cavalry Regiment**
   (Kosakenkreuz des Siber-Reiter-Rgt. Nr. 2)
   ** Original issue enamel and gilt bronze by
   (Croat) Knaub of Zagreb $1,000

Nr. 48

Nr. 49

50. **The P.O.A. (ROA) Vlassov Officer's School Badge c.1941**
   (I. Offizier-Schule der ROA Traditionsabzeichen)
   ** Original issue in grey metal with matt painted center pin-back ... $1,500

Nr. 50

Kapitän zur See Alfred-Karl Smidt wearing the gilt Narvik Campaign Shield.

Nr. 51

51. The Narvik Campaign Shield 1940 (Narvikschild)

(a)	Type A Silver grey metal as issued to the Army, Luftwaffe and Waffen SS	$75
(b)	Type B Matt gilt metal as issued to the Navy	95
(c)	Cloth backing for either Luftwaffe, Army or W-SS	95
(d)	Cloth backing for Naval issue gilt shield	125
(e)	Certificate	125

Besitzzeugnis

In Namen des Führers

wurde dem Jäger Kurt S c h ö n e
4./Fallschirm - Jäger Rgt. 1

der *Narvikschild* verliehen.

(Dienstsiegel)

K.H.Qu., den 1.7.1941.
(Ort und Datum)

General der Gebirgstruppen
Befehlshaber der Gruppe Narvik

Nr. 51(e)

Nr. 52

BESITZZEUGNIS

IM NAMEN
DES FÜHRERS
WURDE DEM

Ofw.
(DIENSTGRAD)

Karl Bluemler
(VOR- UND FAMILIENNAME)

3./M.G.Btl. 10
(TRUPPENTEIL)

DER
CHOLMSCHILD
VERLIEHEN.

O.U. den 31. 10. 42.
(ORT UND DATUM)

GENERALMAJOR

Nr. 52(c)

George Petersen

52. The Cholm Campaign Shield 1942
(Cholmschild)

(a)	Type A	Shield with no backing cloth	$300
(b)	Type B	Shield with cloth backing for Luftwaffe, Army or W-SS	400
(c)		Certificate	250

53. The Crimea Campaign Shield 1941-42
(Krimschild)

(a)	Type A	Early issue in bronze	$40
(b)	Type B	Later type in bronze alloy or tin	40
(c)		Shield with cloth backing for Luftwaffe	75
(d)		Shield with cloth backing for Navy	95
(e)		Shield with cloth backing for Army/W-SS	60
(f)		Certificate	85

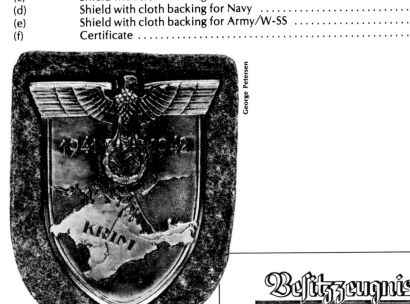

George Petersen

Nr. 53

George Petersen

Befitzzeugnis

IM NAMEN DES FÜHRERS

WURDE DEM

Unteroffozier

(DIENSTGRAD)

Hans Georg Rummler

(VOR u-FAMILIENNAME)

4./Kampfgeschw. 26 (LT)

(TRUPPENTEIL)

Der Krimschild

➤ VERLIEHEN. ◄

H.Qu.,den 3.Oktober 1943

(ORT UND DATUM)

GENERALFELDMARSCHALL

Nr. 53(f)

54. Demjansk Shield 1943
(Demjanskschild)
(a) Type A Shield without any cloth backing $95
(b) Type B Shield with cloth backing for Army/W-SS 125
(c)   Certificate 150

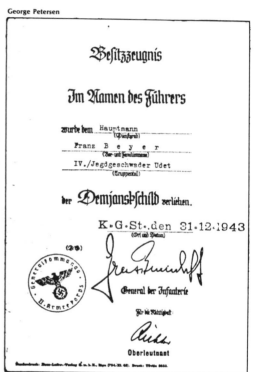

Nr. 54

George Petersen

Nr. 54(c)

55. The Kuban Campaign Shield 1943
(Kubanschild)
(a) Type A Shield without any cloth backing $60
(b) Type B Shield with cloth backing for Luftwaffe 80
(c) Type C Shield with cloth backing for Navy 90
(d) Type D Shield with cloth backing for Army/W-SS 70
(e)   Certificate 90

56. Warsaw Shield 1944
(Warschauschild)
** No shields produced, only a few manufacturers'
sample matrices exist .... *

57. Lorient Shield 1944
(Lorientschild)
** Variations exist in crude materials $250

42

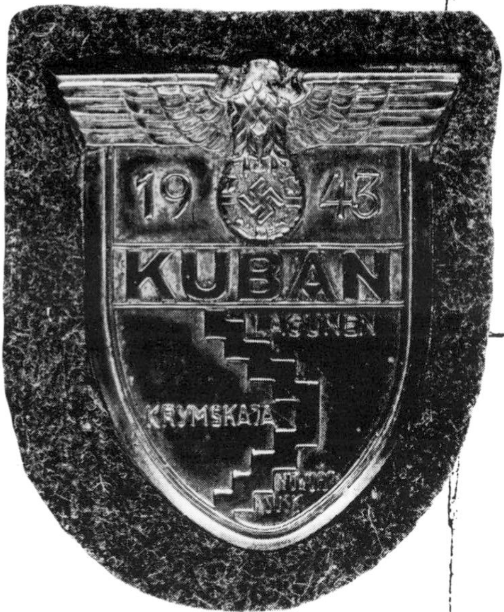

19 43
KUBAN
LAGUNEN
KRYMSKAJA

Nr. 55

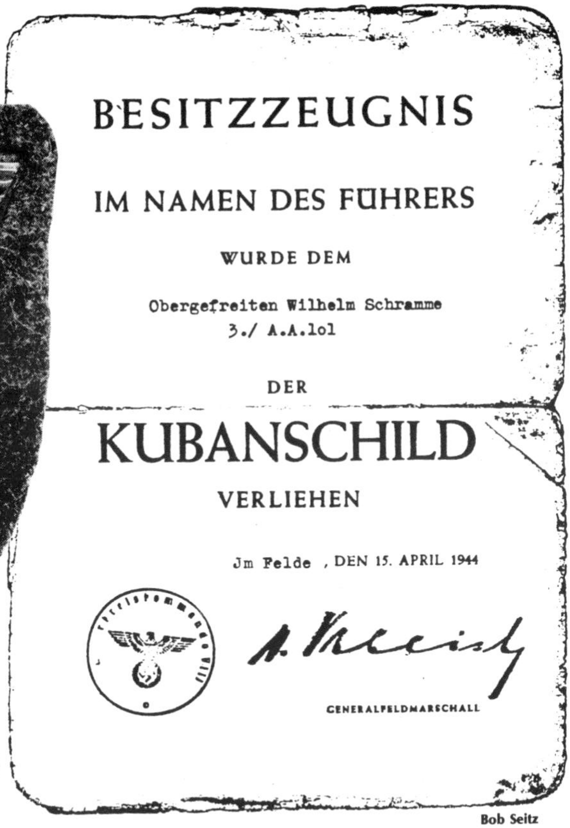

BESITZZEUGNIS

IM NAMEN DES FÜHRERS

WURDE DEM

Obergefreiten Wilhelm Schramme
3./ A.A.lol

DER

KUBANSCHILD

VERLIEHEN

Jm Felde , DEN 15. APRIL 1944

GENERALFELDMARSCHALL

Nr. 55(e)

Bob Seitz

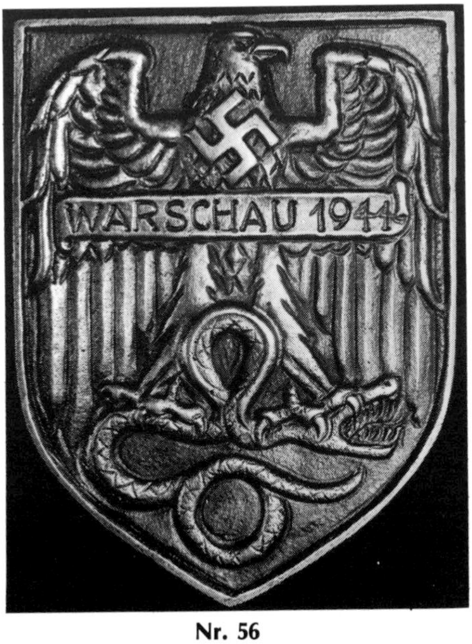

WARSCHAU 1944

Nr. 56

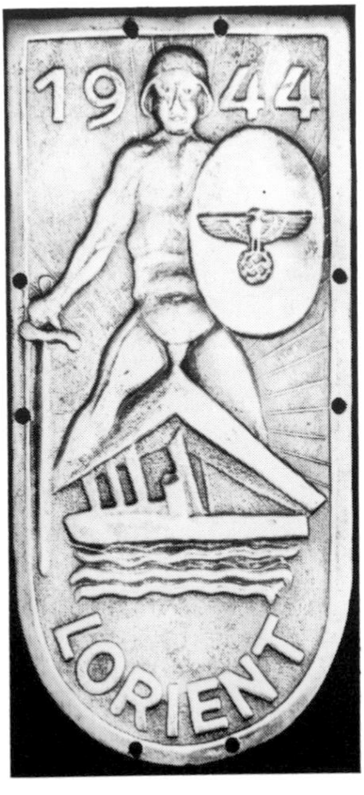

1944
LORIENT

Nr. 57

58. The Lapland Campaign Shield 1945 (Lapplandschild)

(a) **   Variations exist in crude materials $250-350

(b)   Certificate 200-250

Nr. 58

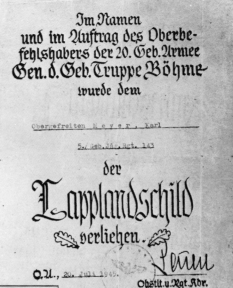

Nr. 58(b)

Nr. 58(b). Typewritten version dated 21 July 1945 and awarded in a POW camp.

44

59. "Crete" Commemorative Cuff Title 1942
    (Ärmelband "Kreta")
(a) Type A Superior quality manufacture with 9-leaf cone $200
(b) Type B Normal issue with 7-leaf cone 150
(c)   Certificate 200

Nr. 59

IM NAMEN DES FÜHRERS
UND OBERSTEN BEFEHLSHABERS
DER WEHRMACHT
VERLEIHE ICH
DAS

ÄRMELBAND »KRETA«

Feldwebel

Ewald   Hermet

O.U.   , DEN   16. Nov.   194 3

DER KOMMANDIERENDE GENERAL
DES XI. FLIEGER-KORPS

Student

GENERAL DER FLIEGER

George Petersen

Nr. 59(c)

60. "Africa" Commemorative Cuff Title 1941
(Ärmelband "Afrika")

(a)	Type A	Afrika Corps issue	$125
(b)	Type B	Luftwaffe issue	150
(c)	Type C	Naval issue	180
(d)		Certificate	200

Nr. 60

George Petersen

Besitzurkunde
Ich verleihe dem

Prüfmeister

Alfred A d e

das

Ärmelband

~ Afrika ~

Hauptquartier des O.B.S., den 1.5.1943   Der Oberbefehlshaber Süd

Keßelring

Generalfeldmarschall

F. d. R.:

Nr. 60(d)

Besitzzeugnis.

Auf Grund der Ermächtigung

des Oberbefehlshabers der Kriegsmarine

verleihe ich dem

Korvettenkapitaen

Hagen K u e s t e r

das **Ärmelband " Afrika „**

R o m, den 6.September 1943

Ort und Datum

Konteradmiral

(Dienstsiegel)   und Befehlshaber des Deutschen

Marinekommandos Italien

Dienstgrad und Dienststellung
des Verleihungsberechtigten

Nr. 60(d), naval issue.

61. "Metz 1944" Cuff Title
(Ärmelband "Metz 1944")
** Instituted by Hitler and manufactured but few awarded $300-350

Hritz

Nr. 61

62. "Courland" Campaign Cuff Title 1944
   (Ärmelband "Kurland")
(a) Type A Superior quality, wide BeVo style silk cotton $400
(b) Type B Cruder variations in cotton, etc. 300
(c)   Certificate 300

Nr. 62

63. Army/Waffen-SS Infantry Assault Badge 1939
   (Infanterie-Sturmabzeichen)
(a) Type A Early quality silver-plated badge $30-35
(b) Type B Later issues in silvered or grey metal or alloy 20-30
(c)   Certificate 60
(d)   Titled paper packet or cardboard carton 20

Nr's. 63 & 64

64. Army/Waffen-SS Infantry Assault Badge Bronze Grade 1940
   (Infanterie-Sturmabzeichen)
(a) Type A Early quality bronze $40
(b) Type B Later issue in bronzed metal or alloy 30
(c)   Certificate 80
(d)   Titled paper packet or cardboard carton 25

65. Army/Waffen-SS Tank Battle Badge in Silver 1939
   (Panzerkampfabzeichen in Silber)
(a) Type A Early silver-plated issue $45
(b) Type B Later issues in silvered or grey metal 35
(c)   Certificate 75
(d)   Titled paper packet or cardboard carton 15

Nr's. 65 & 66

**66. Army/Waffen-SS Tank Battle Badge in Bronze 1940
(Panzerkampfabzeichen in Bronze)**

(a)	Type A	Early bronze issue	$55
(b)	Type B	Later issues in bronzed metal	40
(c)		Certificate	100
(d)		Titled paper packet or cardboard carton	20

**67. Army/Waffen-SS Special Grade of the Tank Battle Badge in Silver
(Panzerkampfabzeichen in Silber mit der Einsatzzahl)**

(a)	Type A	Heavy silver-plated rivetted issued by "JFS" or unmarked	
(b)	Type B	Medium weight silvered rivetted issued by "GB" or unmarked	
(c)		Grade II for 25 Engagements	$350-400
(d)		Grade III for 50 Engagements	500-600
(e)		Grade IV for 75 Engagements	1,500
(f)		Grade V for 100 Engagements	2,000
(g)		Certificates .... From	$200-400-
			800-1200

Nr's. 67(c) & 68(c)   Nr's. 67(d) & 68(d)   49

Nr's. 67(e) & 68(e)   Nr's. 67(f) & 68(f)

68. Army/Waffen-SS Special grade of the Tank Battle Badge in Bronze (Panzerkampfabzeichen in Bronze mit der Einsatzzahl)

(a)	Type A	Heavy quality olive-brown rivetted issue, fine zinc by "JFS" or unmarked	
(b)	Type B	Medium weight rivetted issue by "GB" or unmarked	
(c)		Grade II for 25 Engagements	$450-500
(d)		Grade III for 50 Engagements	700-750
(e)		Grade IV for 75 Engagements	1,800-2,000
(f)		Grade V for 100 Engagements	2,000-2,200
(g)		Certificates	From 250-450- 900-1,400

69. Army/Waffen-SS General Assault Badge 1940 (Allgemeines-Sturmabzeichen)

(a)	Type A	Early silver-plated issue	$40
(b)	Type B	Later issues in silvered or grey metal	30
(c)		Certificate	65
(d)		Titled paper packet or cardboard carton	20

Nr. 69

70. Army/Waffen-SS Special Grade of the General Assault Badge 1943
   (Allgemeines Sturmabzeichen mit der Einsatzzahl)
(a) Type A Heavy silvered-plated rivetted issue by "JFS" or unmarked
(b) Type B Medium weight silvered rivetted issued by "GB" or unmarked
(c)   Grade II for 25 Engagements $350-400
(d)   Grade III for 50 Engagements 500-600
(e)   Grade IV for 75 Engagements 1,500
(f)   Grade V for 100 Engagements 2,000
(g)   Certificates ....From $200-400-
                                                                    700-1100

Nr. 70(c)

Nr. 70(d)

Nr. 70(e)

Nr. 70(f)

71. Army Flak Badge 1941
   (Heeres-Flakabziechen)
(a) Type A Heavy quality oxidized silver-plated issue
             some with maker's mark $150
(b) Type B Later issue in silvered or grey zinc or alloy
             some with maker's mark 120
(c)   Certificate 125
(d)   Titled paper packet or cardboard carton 45   51

**72. Army/Waffen-SS Close Combat Clasp 1942-45
(Nahkampfspange)**

(a) Type A   Heavy, early plated bronze with maker's mark
(b) Type B   Heavy or medium weight with gilt, silver or bronze
           wash on grey zinc or alloy
(c)   Grade I Bronze for 15 Combat Days $70-90
(d)   Grade II Silver for 30 Combat Days 120-150
(e)   Grade III Gold for 50 Combat Days 250-600
(f)   Certificates ....From $60-90-600
(g)   Titled paper packets or cardboard cartons
           for Grades I & II 40-60
(h)   Blue case for Grade III presented by
           Reichsführer-SS in 1944-45 400

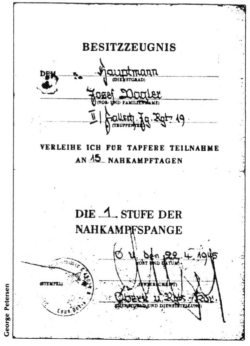

George Petersen

Nr. 72(f)

Nr. 72

Oberst Robert Kaestner wears the Close Combat Clasp on his left breast.

73. Army Parachutist's Badge 1937-45
(Fallschirmschutzen-Abzeichen des Heeres)
(a) Type A First issue deluxe quality in lightweight aluminum $600
(b) Type B Heavy quality metal - later issues of the war 400-500
(c)   Certificate 500-750
(d) Type C Other Rank's type in machine-embroidered (late war) cotton . 400

Nr. 73(b)

VERLEIHUNGSURKUNDE

Ich verleihe dem

Obergefreiten Karl B ü t t n e r

Dienſtgrad, Vor- und Zuname

Fallschirm-Infanterie-Kompanie

Truppenteil

das

Fallſchirmſchützenabzeichen

Dienſt-
ſtempel

Der Oberbefehlshaber des Heeres

Im Auftrage

Nr. der Urkunde

Generalleutnant und Inſpekteur der Infanterie

Berlin, den 1.9.37

Nr. 73(d)

K. Peters

George Petersen

Oberleutnant Alfred Schwarzmann wearing the Army Parachutist's Badge.

74. **Anti-Partisan War Badge**
   (Bandenkampfabzeichen/1944-45)

(a) Type A First issue in zinc manufactured by "Juncker" with stylized skull, cut out serpents and flat pin, semi-hollow reverse

(b) Type B Later issues of the Juncker type, solid serpents, needle pin and another manufacturer's variation with small skull, massive badge, solid back and needle pin

(c) Grade I Bronze for 20 Combat Days $300
(d) Grade II Silver for 50 Combat Days 600
(e) Grade III Gold for 150 Combat Days 800
(f) Certificates .... From $1250-2500-5000
(g) Blue case for Grade III, presented by Reichsführer-SS in 1945 500

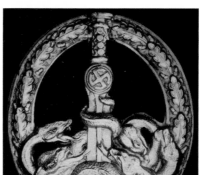

Nr. 74

*Only four gold badges were, in fact, personally awarded by Himmler at his Headquarters on 15 February 1945. These badges were specially made and hand-finished by "Juncker" of Berlin. Deluxe quality convex gold-plated brass with blued steel finish blade and finely detailed cut-out serpents. Wide silver pin on reverse. Most collections have examples of the Gold class but obviously these are manufacturer's or military tailor's examples. The above prices apply to these badges and not to the four specially awarded unique badges and certificates. To date, the only known example of the four presented badges is that illustrated in Bender's Littlejohn and Dodkins, Vol. II, and described by Doctor K.G. Klietmann's book Deutsche Auszeichnunge, Vol. II.

**Special Grade of the Anti-Partisan war badge in Gold with Diamonds 1944-45 (Bandenkampfabzeichen mit Brillanten)

75. **Special Grade of the Anti-Partisan War Badge in Gold with Diamonds 1944-45**
   (Bandenkampfabzeichen mit Brillanten)
   ** Twenty examples in silver gilt with precious stones were manufactured but not awarded .... *

76. Army Balloon Observer's Badge 1944
(Ballonbeobachterabzeichen des Heeres)

(a)	Grade I Bronze for 20 Points	$900
(b)	Grade II Silver for 45 Points	1200
(c)	Grade III Gold for 75 Points - doubtful if awarded	*
(d)	Certificates	From $600-750

Nr. 76

77. Special Badge for Single-Handed Destruction of a Tank 1942-43
(Sonderabzeichen für das Niederkämpfen von Panzerkampfwagen durch Einzelkämpfer)

(a)	Grade I Silver for 1 tank (four such badges could be worn)	$150
(b)	Grade II Gold for 5 tanks	500
(c)	Certificates	From 250-500

Hitler awards Joachim Peiper with the Knight's Cross of the Iron Cross in the Spring of 1943. Note tank destruction badge on his upper right sleeve.

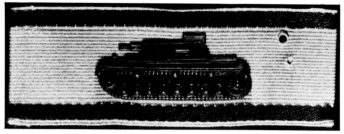

Nr. 77

Belitzzeugnis

Ich verleihe dem

Unteroffizier Ferdinand J ä c k l e

4./Flaksturmregt.20 (mot.)

das

Sonderabzeichen für das Niederkämpfen von Panzerkampfwagen ufw. durch Einzelkämpfer

Hauptquartier des Ob. d. L., den 8. Nov. 194 4

Der Reichsminister der Luftfahrt und Oberbefehlshaber der Luftwaffe

Göring.

Reichsmarschall

Die erfolgte Verleihung wird beglaubigt:
Der Chef des Luftwaffenperfonalamts

Generaloberst

(Dienstfiegel)

Nr. 77(c)

78. Special Badge for Shooting Down Low-Flying Aircraft 1945
   (Tieffliegervernichtungsabzeichen)
   **   Doubtful if awarded
(a)   Grade I Silver for 1 plane ....   *
(b)   Grade II Gold for 5 planes ....   *

Nr. 78

79. The Sniper's Badge 1944-45
   (Scharfschutzenabzeichen)
(a)   3rd Class for 20 Kills $350
(b)   2nd Class for 40 Kills 500
(c)   1st Class for 60 Kills 600
(d)   Certificates .... From $400-500-600
This badge is extremely rare and original examples are rarely
         found in collections, although many copies exist.

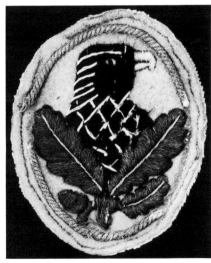

Nr. 79

George Petersen

A German sniper
in action.

80. The Führer Commendation Certificate 1944-45
(Anerkennungsurkunde des Führers)

.... $1500

ICH SPRECHE DER
⚡-PANZER-AUFKLÄRUNGS-
ABTEILUNG 10
FÜR DEN ABSCHUSS VON
DREI FEINDLICHEN FLUGZEUGEN
BEI KURDWANOWKA
AM 6. 4. 1944
MEINE
BESONDERE ANERKENNUNG AUS.

HAUPTQUARTIER·DEN 1. AUGUST 1944

DER FÜHRER

Nr. 80

81. Army Bergführer Badge 1936
(Heeresbergführer)

.... $1400-1700

Nr. 81

82. The Armed Forces (Wehrmacht) Wound Badges 1936-1945
   (Verwundeten-ABZ)

(a) Type A   The so-called Spanish Issue, hollow backed WWI style
             helmet, embossed with swastika.
             Variations of manufacture exist.
(b)   1st Class in Gold. Not awarded during Spanish Civil War $200-250
(c)   2nd Class in Silver. Only one awarded during Spanish Civil War . 150-200
(d)   3rd Class in Black. Only 182 awarded during Spanish Civil War . 75-125
(e)   Certificates awarded for Spanish Civil War .... From $150-300

Nr. 82(a)
(cut-out
variation)

Nr's. 82(b), (c)
   & (d)

George Petersen

NOTE:
Many examples of this early pattern were made
and privately purchased after the Spanish Civil
War had ended.

(f) Type B   1939 Issue with M35 pattern steel helmet
             design. Early badges solid brass or nickel,
             later types in dull zinc.
(g)   1st Class in Gold   75
(h)   Certificate   150
(i)   2nd Class in Silver   45
(j)   Certificate   75
(k)   3rd Class in Black   15
(l)   Certificate   45
(m)   Cases or boxes   30
(n)   Titled paper packets   15

Nr's. 82(g), (i) & (k)

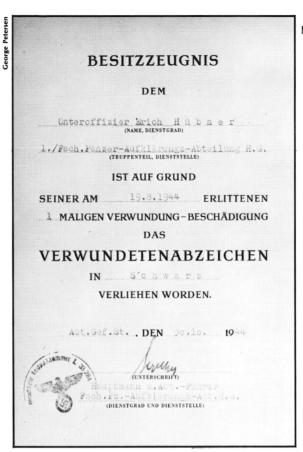

George Petersen

BESITZZEUGNIS

DEM

Unteroffizier Erich H ü b n e r
(NAME, DIENSTGRAD)

1./Fsch.Panzer-Aufklärungs-Abteilung H.G.
(TRUPPENTEIL, DIENSTSTELLE)

IST AUF GRUND

SEINER AM   19.3.1944   ERLITTENEN

1 MALIGEN VERWUNDUNG – BESCHÄDIGUNG

DAS

VERWUNDETENABZEICHEN

IN   S'chwarz

VERLIEHEN WORDEN.

Abt.Gef.St. , DEN   30.10.   19 44

(UNTERSCHRIFT)

Hauptmann u.Abt.-Führer
Fsch.Pz.-Aufklärungs-Abt.H.G.
(DIENSTGRAD UND DIENSTSTELLE)

**83. The Wound Badge for 20th July 1944
(Verwundeten-Abz. 20. Juli. 1944)**

(a) Type A All class issued & presented by Hitler
Manufactured by C.E. Juncker of Berlin. Reverse: hallmarked "800" &
"L/I2." Approx. 100 badges struck $7,500

(b) Presentation Award Document in Folder (All Classes) 12,500

(c) Type B These badges appear to be the DUPLA or
duplicate badges, thus reverse marked "2" &
hallmarked "800." (By Juncker Berlin) 5,000

Nr. 83(a)

Nr. 83(c)

IM NAMEN
DES DEUTSCHEN VOLKES
VERLEIHE ICH DEM
GENERALOBERST
GÜNTHER KORTEN
CHEF DES GENERALSTABES DER LUFTWAFFE
AUF GRUND SEINER AM 20. JULI 1944
ERLITTENEN DRITTEN VERWUNDUNG
DAS
VERWUNDETENABZEICHEN
IN GOLD

FÜHRER-HAUPTQUARTIER, DEN 20. JULI 1944

DER FÜHRER

Nr. 83(b)

Hitler personally presents the special July 20 Wound Badge and certificate to recipients.

84. The Armed Forces (Wehrmacht) Drivers Proficiency Badge (Kraftfahr-Bewährungsabzeichen) 1942-45

(a)	1st Class in Gold	$20-25
(b)	Certificate	85-100
(c)	2nd Class in Silver	15-20
(d)	Certificate	45-60
(e)	3rd Class in Bronze	10-15
(f)	Certificate	40

* Examples issued on cloth backing (Luftwaffe, Navy, & Army) are more scarce than badges with pins. The above prices apply to those with cloth backing.

Nr. 84

Nr. 84(f)

85. Navy U-Boat War Badge 1939 (U-Boots-Kriegsabzeichen)

(a)	Type A Heavy early quality gold-plated bronze issued by "Schwerin" of Berlin or other makers. Some badges unmarked	$150-200
(b)	Type B Later issues in gilt wash on metal or zinc	75-95
(c)	Certificate	150
(d)	Titled paper packet or cardboard carton	From 35-50

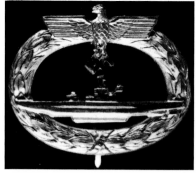

Nr. 85

Verleihungs-Urkunde.

Auf Grund der Ermächtigung des Oberbefehlshabers
der Kriegsmarine verleihe ich dem

Fähnrich zur See
(Dienstgrad)

Hans Hildebrandt
(Name)

das

Ubootskriegsabzeichen 1939

Befehlsstelle , den 17. September 1941

Vizeadmiral und Befehlshaber der Unterseeboote

Nr. 85(c)

86. **Naval U-Boat War Badge with Diamonds**
 (U-Boots-Kriegsabzeichen mit Brillanten)
(a) Type A Fine quality gold-plated silver badge with diamonds
  on Swastika by "Schwerin" of Berlin $10,000
(b) Type B Jeweller's manufacture dress copy in gold-plated
  silver with semi-precious stones 5,000
(c) Type C Unique superb presentation badge awarded to
  Grand Admiral Dönitz in solid gold with diamonds inset
  on wreath and swastika . . . . *
(d) Large presentation document in folder 18,000

Nr. 86

87. Navy U-Boat Combat Clasp 1944-45
(U-Boots-Frontspange)

(a) Type A Heavy quality silver or bronze-plated brass by "Schwerin" and "Peekhaus" with flat tapered pin.

(b) Type B Medium weight silvered or bronzed metal or zinc by "Schwerin" and "Peekhaus" with fluted tapered pin.

(c)   Bronze Class for either bravery or several missions $300-350

(d)   Silver Class for either bravery or several missions 450

(e)   Certificates .... From 200-300

Nr. 87

88. Naval Destroyer's War Badge 1940
(Zerstörer-Kriegsabzeichen)

(a) Type A Heavy quality silver/gold-plated brass by
"Schwerin" of Berlin $125-150

(b) Type B Medium weight silvered/gilt wash metal or zinc,
some with maker's mark 75-95

(c)   Certificate 100-150

(d)   Titled paper packet or cardboard carton .... From 35-50

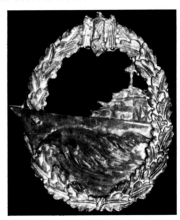

Nr. 88

Nr. 88(c)

67

89. Naval Minesweepers, Sub-Chasers & Escort Vessels War Badge 1940
   (Kriegsabzeichen für Minensuch, U-Boots-Jagd, und Sicherungsverbände)
   (a) Type A Heavy quality silver/gold-plated brass by
                "Schwerin" of Berlin $125
   (b) Type B Medium weight silvered/gilt wash metal or zinc,
                some with maker's mark 75
   (c)   Certificate 75
   (d)   Titled paper packet or cardboard carton .... From 30-40

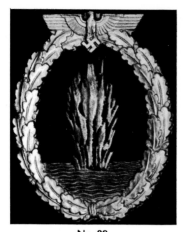

Nr. 89

VERLEIHUNGS-URKUNDE

Im Namen
des Oberbefehlshabers
der Kriegsmarine verleihe ich dem

Maschinisten   Hans   S t o r c h
                (Dienstgrad, Name)

das

Kriegsabzeichen

für

Minensuch-, Ubootsjagd- und

Sicherungsverbände

*

St. Qu.   , den 6. Juli   1942

Kpt. z. See
und Führer der 1. Sicherungsdivision

Nr. 89(c)

90. Naval 1st Pattern E-Boat War Badge 1942-43
   (Schnellboot-Kriegsabzeichen)
   (a) Type A Heavy quality silver/gold-plated brass by
                "Schwerin" of Berlin $450
   (b) Type B Medium weight silvered/gilt wash metal or zinc,
                some with maker's mark 300
   (c)   Certificate 250
   (d)   Titled paper packet or cardboard carton 100

Nr. 90   Nr. 91

91. Naval 2nd Pattern E-Boat War Badge 1943-45
(Schnellboot-Kreigsabzeichen)

(a) Type A Heavy quality silver/gilt wash on metal or zinc by
"Schwerin" of Berlin. Rarely found with gilt finish $150
(b) Type B Heavy quality silver/gilt wash on metal with maker's
mark, "A.S." needle pin 150
(c) Certificate 150
(d) Titled paper packet or cardboard carton .... From 50-60

92. Naval E-Boat War Badge with Diamonds
(Schnellboot-Kriegsabzeichen mit Brillanten)

(a) Type A Fine quality gold-plated, hallmarked silver badge inset with
tiny diamonds on the swastika. Manufactured by "Schwerin".. $10,000
(b) Type B Jeweller's manufacture dress copy in gold-plated silver
with semi-precious stones 5,000
(c) Large presentation document in folder 10,000
(d) Presentation blue case 400

Nr. 92

93. Naval Auxiliary Cruisers War Badge 1941
(Kriegsabzeichen für Hilfskreuzer)

(a) Type A Heavy quality silver/gold-plated, rivetted badge
by "Schwerin" $150-175

(b) Type B Mid-war issue, gilt wash on metal or zinc, rivetted 75-95

(c) Type C Late war issue, gilt wash on grey zinc.
No rivet, needle pin 50

(d)   Certificate 200

(e)   Titled paper packet or cardboard carton 50

Nr. 93

BESITZZEUGNIS

Jm Namen
des Oberbefehlshabers
der Kriegsmarine

verleihe ich

dem

Obermaschinenmaat d. Res.

S t o r c h

das

Kriegsabzeichen für Hilfskreuzer

Bordeaur, den 25. August 1941

Fregattenkapitän
und Kommandant

Mohawk Arms

Nr. 93(d)

Nr. 94

94. Naval Auxiliary Cruisers War Badge with Diamonds
(Kreigsabzeichen für Hilfskreuzer mit Brillanten)

(a) Type A Fine quality gold-plated, hallmarked silver badge inset with
tiny diamonds on the swastika. Manufactured by "Schwerin"..$12,500

(b) Type B Jeweller's manufacture dress copy in gold-plated silver
with semi-precious stones 5,000

(c)   Large presentation document in folder 12,500

(d)   Presentation blue case 400

95. Naval High Seas Fleet War Badge 1941
(Flotten-Kriegsabzeichen)

(a)	Type A	Heavy quality silver/gold-plated brass by Adolf Bock	$150
(b)	Type B	Late war issue gilt wash on grey zinc, needle or flat pin, some with maker's mark	50-75
(c)		Certificate	100-150
(d)		Titled paper packet or cardboard carton, also blue case for early badge	From 40-60

Nr. 95

Im Namen des Oberbefehlshabers
der Kriegsmarine

verleihe ich dem

Leutnant (Ing.)

Paul Weidlich

für die Teilnahme an den Kriegsfahrten des

Schlachtschiff „Scharnorst"

das

Flotten-Kriegsabzeichen

Den 1... Mrz 1942.

... Befehlshaber der Schlachtschiffe

In Vertretung!

Kapitän zur See

Nr. 95(c)

Nr. 96

96. Navy High Seas Fleet War Badge with Diamonds
(Flotten-Kreigsabzeichen mit Brillanten)

(a)	Type A	Fine quality gold-plated, hallmarked silver badge, large swastika inset with tiny diamonds	$10,000
(b)	Type B	Jeweller's manufacture dress copy in gold-plated silver with semi-precious stones	5,000
(c)		Large presentation document in folder	10,000
(d)		Presentation blue case	400

Admiral Oskar Kummetz wears the High Seas Fleet War Badge.

Im Namen des
Führers und Obersten Befehlshabers
der Wehrmacht

verleihe ich

dem

Sa. Ob. Gefreiten

Friedrich Strunk

das

Abzeichen für Blockadebrecher

Den ___25. August___ 19 _44_

Der Oberbefehlshaber der Kriegsmarine

Dönitz
Großadmiral

Für die Richtigkeit:

Kapitän z.S. u. Abtlg.-Chef

Dienstgrad und Dienststellung

Nr. 97(c)

97. Naval Blockade Runners Badge 1941
(Abzeichen für Blockadebrecher)

(a) Type A Early heavy quality oxidized silver-plated brass
                 by Adolf Bock, wide tapered pin $135-150

(b) Type B Heavy oxidized silvered metal, needle pin,
                 some with maker's mark 90-100

(c)   Certificate 150

(d)   Large blue case for badge and miniature stickpin 40

(e)   Blue case for badge 40

(f)   Large half-size miniature of badge on stickpin 60

Nr. 97

Nr. 98(a)

Nr. 98(c)

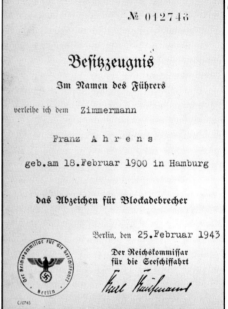

D. Frailey

№ 012746

Besitzzeugnis

Im Namen des Führers

verleihe ich dem   Zimmermann

Franz   Ahrens

geb. am 18. Februar 1900 in Hamburg

das Abzeichen für Blockadebrecher

Berlin, den 25. Februar 1943

Der Reichskommissar
für die Seeschiffahrt

Nr. 97(c)

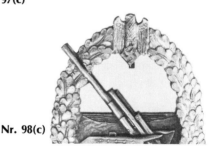

98. Naval Coastal Artillery War Badge 1941
(Kriegsabzeichen für die Marine Artillerie)

(a) Type A Early quality plated/brass by "Schwerin"
                 tapered pin $125

(b) Type B Late war issue, needle pin 45-60

(c) Type C Variation, "Small Eagle" type 100

(d)   Certificate 100

(e)   Titled paper packet 25

(f)   Titled blue case 50

1941   Nr. 98(d)

Im Namen
des
Oberbefehlshabers
der
Kriegsmarine
verleihe ich

dem ̲M̲.̲A̲.̲M̲a̲a̲t̲ ̲H̲i̲l̲l̲e̲_̲e̲i̲s̲t̲,̲ ̲K̲a̲r̲l̲

das
Kriegsabzeichen
für die
Marine-Artillerie

Marinebefehlshaber
Kanalküste

Den 1.10.1942.   Admiral

99. Naval Close Combat Clasp 1944-45
    (Marine-Frontspange)
**   Crude originals exist & manufacturer's samples
       in brass $250-400

Nr. 99

100. Naval Combat Badge of the Small Battle Units (K-Men) 1943
    (Kampfabzeichen der Kleinkampfmittel)

(a)	1st Class, gold metal clasp (not awarded)	*
(b)	2nd Class, silver metal clasp (not awarded)	*
(c)	3rd Class, bronze metal clasp	$400
(d)	4th Class, cloth patch (3 swords)	250
(e)	5th Class, patch (2 swords)	200
(f)	6th Class, cloth patch (1 sword)	200
(g)	7th Class, cloth patch (no swords)	150

Nr. 100(a), (b) & (c)

Nr. 100(d)

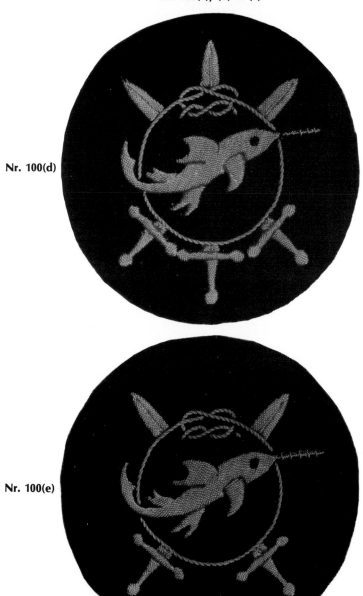

Nr. 100(e)

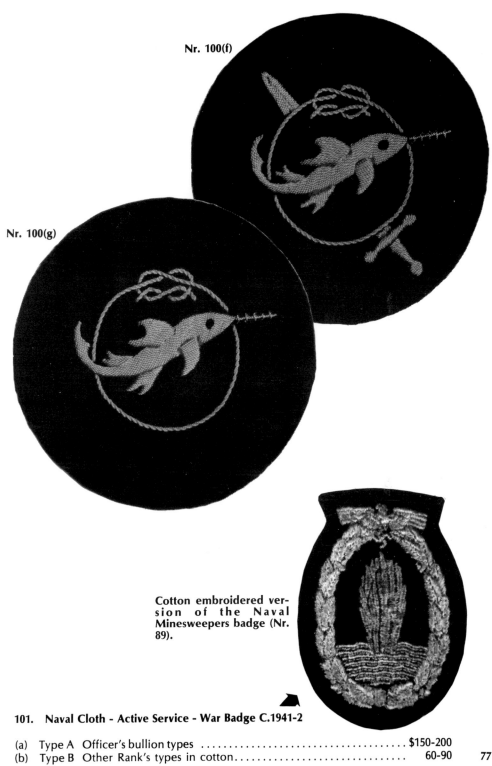

Nr. 100(f)

Nr. 100(g)

Cotton embroidered version of the Naval Minesweepers badge (Nr. 89).

101. Naval Cloth - Active Service - War Badge C.1941-2

(a) Type A Officer's bullion types $150-200
(b) Type B Other Rank's types in cotton.............................. 60-90

102. Luftwaffe Aircrew Badge 1935-36
(Fliegerschaftsabzeichen)

Examples exist by "Juncker" of Berlin and "Godet" of Berlin

(a) Type A Wide flat hallmarked pin $1500-2000
(b) Type B Normal tapered pin 1500
(c)   Certificate 600
(d)   Titled blue case 300

Nr. 102(a)

103. Luftwaffe Pilot's Badge 1936-45
(Flugzeugführerabzeichen)

(a) Type A Early quality plated type $300
(b) Type B War-time issues 250
(c) Type C Very late war issues in alloy (crude) 125
(d)   Certificate 75-100
(e)   Titled blue case 75-100

Nr. 103

Verleihungsurkunde

Ich verleihe dem

Feldwebel (d.Res.)

Heinz Fracht

das Abzeichen für

Flugzeugführer

Berlin, den 23. Juni 194 2

Der Reichsminister der Luftfahrt
und Oberbefehlshaber der Luftwaffe
I. A.:
Der Chef des Luftwaffenpersonalamts

R. 104 141 H 2

General der Flieger

George Petersen

Nr. 103(d)

78

104. Luftwaffe Observer's Badge 1936-45 (Beobachterabzeichen)

(a) Type A Early quality plated type $300
(b) Type B War-time issues 250
(c) Type C Very late war issues (crude) in alloy 125
(d)   Certificate 100-150
(e)   Titled blue case 75-100

Nr. 104

George Petersen

Nr. 104(e)

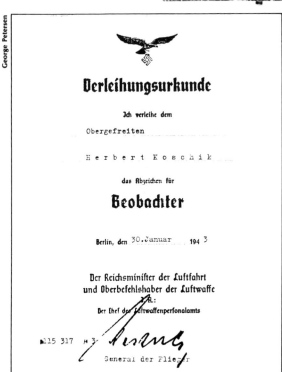

George Petersen

Verleihungsurkunde

Ich verleihe dem

Obergefreiten

Herbert Koschik

das Abzeichen für

Beobachter

Berlin, den 30. Januar 194 3

Der Reichsminister der Luftfahrt
und Oberbefehlshaber der Luftwaffe
J.A.:
Der Chef des Luftwaffenpersonalamts

115 317 H 3

General der Flieger

Nr. 104(d)

105. Luftwaffe Combined Pilot/Observer Badge 1936-45
(Gemeinsames Flugzeugführer-und Beobachter-Abzeichen)

(a)	Type A	Early quality plated/brass type	$600-750
(b)	Type B	War-time issues	350
(c)	Type C	Very late war issued marked "A" in alloy	250
(d)		Certificate	300
(e)		Titled blue case	75-150

Nr. 105

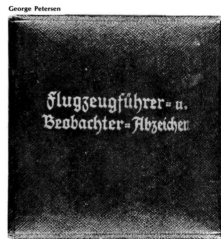

Nr. 105(e)

Nr. 105(d)

106. Luftwaffe Special Combined Pilot/Observer Badge with Diamonds
   (Gemeinsamesflugzeugführer und Beobachter Abzeichen in Gold mit Brillanten)

(a) Type A Actual award badge in solid gold & platinum
              with diamonds $12,500
(b) Type B Officially awarded dress copy in silver/gilt with
              sapphires by "Rudolf Sturk" of Vienna 7,500
(c)   Award document in folder and outer case 7,500
(d)   Presentation blue case for badge 500

Nr. 106

Field Marshal Erhard Milch wearing
the Combined Pilot/Observer Badge
with Diamonds.

107. Luftwaffe Wireless Operator/Air Gunners Badge 1936-45
   (Fliegerschützenabzeichen für Bordfunker)

(a) Type A Early quality plated/brass type $250-300
(b) Type B War-time issues 150
(c) Type C Late war issues (solid swastika detail) in alloy 100
(d)   Certificate 125
(e)   Titled blue case 75-125

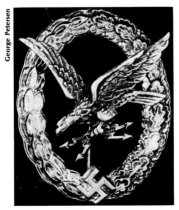

Nr. 107

108. Luftwaffe Air-Gunners/Flight Engineers Badge 1942-45
   (Fliegerschützenabzeichen für Bordschützen u.Bordmechaniker)
(a)   Type A Early quality plated badge C.1942 ....$300-350
(b)   Type B War-time issues 1943 200
(c)   Type C Late war issue 1944-45 (solid swastika detail)
             in alloy 150
(d)   Certificate 150
(e)   Titled blue case 75-125

Nr. 108

109. Luftwaffe Glider Pilot Badge 1940
   (Segelflugzeugführerabzeichen)
(a)   Type A Early quality plated badge of "Juncker" $1,200
(b)   Type B Middle war-time issues (plated metal) 600
(c)   Type C Late war issued (solid swastika detail) zinc 350
(d)   Certificate 1,000
(e)   Titled blue case 200-250

George Petersen

Nr. 109

George Petersen

Segel=
Flugzeugführer=
Abzeichen

Nr. 109(e)

110. **Luftwaffe Flier's Commemorative Badge 1936-45**
(Flieger-Erinnerungsabzeichen)
(a)	Type A Early quality plated badge by "Juncker"	$1,500
(b)	Type B War-time issue plated metal	600
(c)	Type C Late war issue (solid swastika detail) in zinc	350
(d)	Certificate	1,000
(e)	Titled blue case	200-250

Nr. 110

George Petersen

Verleihungsurkunde

Ich verleihe dem

Unteroffizier

K a r l   S t o f f l

das

Fliegererinnerungsabzeichen

Berlín, den 1.November 194 3

Der Reichsminister der Luftfahrt
und Oberbefehlshaber der Luftwaffe
J. A.:
Der Chef des Luftwaffenperfonalamts

Nr. 403 /43

Generaloberst

Nr. 110(d)

83

(Z w e i t s c h r i f t)

Verleihungsurkunde

Ich verleihe dem

Flieger

Johannes F r a h m

das Abzeichen für

Fliegerschützen
(mit Blitzbündel)

Berlin, den   25.Mai   194 2

Der Reichsminister der Luftfahrt
und Oberbefehlshaber der Luftwaffe
J. A.:
Der Chef des Luftwaffenpersonalamts
gez. Kastner

General der Flieger

F.d.R.

Oberstleutnant

Nr. 101537 /42
Berlin, den 28.7.42

nr. 90

Nr. 107(d)

George Petersen

Verleihungsurkunde

Ich verleihe dem

Unteroffizier

H e i n z   P r a h m

das Abzeichen für

Fliegerſchützen
ohne Blitzbündel

Berlín, den 29. Juli 194 2

Der Reichsminiſter der Luftfahrt
und Oberbefehlshaber der Luftwaffe
J. A.:
Der Chef des Luftwaffenperſonalamts

Nr. 1o5 927

General der Flieger

Nr. 108(d)

Verleihungsurkunde

Ich verleihe dem

Unteroffizier

Fritz Haas

das Abzeichen für

Fliegerschützen

mit Blitzbündel

Berlin, den 25. November 1943

Der Reichsminister der Luftfahrt
und Oberbefehlshaber der Luftwaffe
J. A.:
Der Chef des Luftwaffenpersonalamts

Nr. 148 889 /43   Generaloberst

Nr. 107(d)

Note: The documents on the previous two pages with typed-in "mit" and "ohne"
were used until these preprinted versions were made available.

Verleihungsurkunde

Ich verleihe dem

Unteroffizier

A d o l f   M a r t e n s

das Abzeichen für

Fliegerſchützen

ohne Blitzbündel

Berlin, den 11.November 194 3

Der Reichsminiſter der Luftfahrt
und Oberbefehlshaber der Luftwaffe
J. A.:
Der Chef des Luftwaffenperſonalamts

Nr. 146 792 /43

Generaloberst

Nr. 108(d)

111. Luftwaffe Flak War Badge 1941-45
(Flak-Kampfabzeichen der Luftwaffe)
(a) Type A Early quality plated badge with maker's mark $125
(b) Type B Late war issue 60-85
(c)   Certificate 100
(d)   Titled black carton box 75
(e)   Titled blue case 100-125

Nr. 111

Nr. 111(e)

George Petersen

Nr. 111(c)

112. Luftwaffe Ground Combat Badge 1942-45
(Erdkampfabzeichen der Luftwaffe)
(a)   Type A Early quality plated badge by "M.u.K" (two-part) $125-150
(b)   Type B Middle war-time issue (two-part) plated metal 80-100
(c)   Type C Late war issued (one-part) zinc 60
(d)   Certificate 100
(e)   Titled blue case 150-200

Nr. 112

Nr. 112(e)

Befitzeugnis

Dem

Unteroffizier
(Dienstgrad)

Erich H ü b n e r
(Vor- und Familienname)

Pz.Aufkl.Abt.H.G.
(Truppenteil)

verleihe ich das

Erdkampfabzeichen der Luftwaffe

St.Qu.,22.Nov.1943
(Ort und Datum)
Für das Divisionskommando:
I.A.

Hauptmann und Adjutant
(Dienstgrad und Dienststellung)

1343 Maximilian-Verlag, Berlin SW 68, Ritterstr. 33 4.43.

Nr. 112(d)

113. Luftwaffe Special Grade Ground Combat Badge 1944-45 (Erdkampfabzeichen der Luftwaffe - Sonder Klasse)

(a)   "100" Engagements .... *
(b)   "75" Engagements .... *
(c)   "50" Engagements .... *
(d)   "25" Engagements .... *
(e)   Certificates .... *

D. Littlejohn

Nr. 113(a)   Nr. 113(b)

114. Luftwaffe Tank Battle Badge & Special Grade Badges (Panzerkampfabzeichen der Luftwaffe)

(a)   Tank Battle Badge - unnumbered .... *
(b)   "100" Engagements .... *
(c)   "75" Engagements .... *
(d)   "50" Engagements .... *
(e)   "25" Engagements .... *
(f)   Certificates .... *

Nr. 114(a)   Nr. 114(c)

Feldwebel Karl Otte wears the Luftwaffe Ground Combat badge as a member of the Hermann Göring Division, Italy, 1944.

George Petersen

115. Luftwaffe Sea Battle Badge 1944
(Seekampfabzeichen der Luftwaffe)

(a) **   Very few awarded .... *
(b)   Certificate .... *

Nr. 115

116. Luftwaffe Close Combat Clasp 1944
(Nahkampfspange der Luftwaffe)

(a)		Class I bronze	....	*
(b)	**	Class II silver	....	*
(c)		Class III gold	....	*
(d)		Certificate	....	1000-1500

Only a few badges actually awarded.

The illustrated
example is a
current copy.

Nr. 116

Klaus Peters

B e s i t z z e u g n i s

In Namen des

Oberbefehlshabers der Luftwaffe

verleihe ich

dem

Feldwebel

Georg W e l t e r

I./Fallsch.Pz.Gren.Rgt. 3 HG

die

Nahkampfspange der Luftwaffe

in B r o n z e

Gefechtsstand, den 24. 2. 1945

Oberstleutnant u. Rgt.-Kdr.

Nr. 116(d)

117. Luftwaffe Parachutist's Badge 1936-45
(Fallschirmschützenabzeichen)

(a)	Type A	Early quality plated brass badge with maker's stamp	$250
(b)	Type B	War-time issues, plated metal	150-200
(c)	Type C	Late war issues in zinc, etc.	120
(d)		Certificate	150
(e)		Titled blue case	75-100

Nr. 117

Oberstlt. Walter Koch wears the Parachutist's Badge, the Ground Combat Badge and the Pilot's Badge.

Three variations of the case (Nr. 117(e)) for the Parachutist's Badge.

93

VERLEIHUNGSURKUNDE

IM NAMEN DES
OBERBEFEHLSHABERS DER LUFTWAFFE
VERLEIHE ICH DEM

Dienstgrad

Vor- und Zuname

DAS ABZEICHEN FÜR

FALLSCHIRMS CHÜTZEN

Gef. Stand, den   16. Juli 1944
Fallschirm-Armee-Oberkommando
Der Oberbefehlshaber
I.V.

Generalleutnant

290/44

Two variations of the certificate (Nr. 117(d)) for the Parachutist's Badge.

Verleihungsurkunde

Ich verleihe dem

Jäger

Alois Huber

das Abzeichen für

Fallschirmschützen

Berlin, den 18. März   1941

Der Reichsminister der Luftfahrt
und Oberbefehlshaber der Luftwaffe
I. A.:
Der Chef des Luftwaffenpersonalamts

III   M 1/   Generalleutnant

Note:
Luftwaffe personnel utilized cloth versions of their war badges more than any other branch of service, variations of which are illustrated below.

(a)   Officer's Bullion types $150-300
(b)   Other Rank's types in cotton 30-60

Nr. 103 (bullion)

Nr. 104 (bullion)

Nr. 105 (bullion)

Nr. 107 (bullion)

95

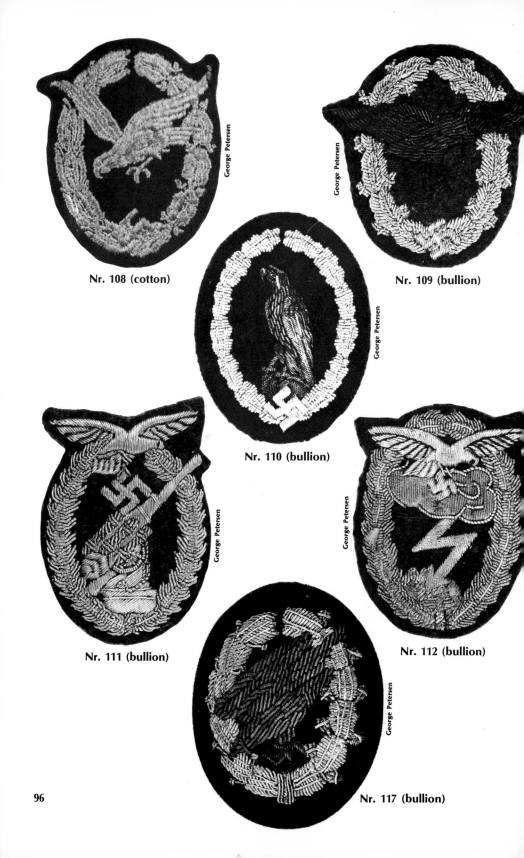

Nr. 108 (cotton)

Nr. 109 (bullion)

Nr. 110 (bullion)

Nr. 111 (bullion)

Nr. 112 (bullion)

Nr. 117 (bullion)

George Petersen

118. Luftwaffe Day Fighter Clasp 1941-45
(Frontflugspange für Jäger)

(a)	Gold Class with Pendant (numbered missions)	$450-700
(b)	Certificate	350-500
(c)	Gold Class with Pendant (flower design)	450-550
(d)	Certificate	300-350
(e)	Gold Class	300-350
(f)	Certificate	250-300
(g)	Silver Class	250-300
(h)	Certificate	250
(i)	Bronze Class	200-250
(j)	Certificate	200

*Prices apply to only early quality clasps, late war issues
in zinc (crude) would be priced at some 30% less.

(k)	Titled blue cases	125-150

Nr. 118

Nr. 118(c)

119. Luftwaffe Night Fighter Clasp 1941-45 (black wreath)
(Frontflugspange für Nachtjäger)

(a)	Gold Class with Pendant (numbered missions)	$450-750
(b)	Certificate	350-400
(c)	Gold Class with Pendant (flower design)	450-550
(d)	Certificate	350
(e)	Gold Class	350
(f)	Certificate	300
(g)	Silver Class	250
(h)	Certificate	200
(i)	Bronze Class	200
(j)	Certificate	150

*Prices apply to only early quality clasps, late war issues
in zinc (crude) would be priced at some 30% less.

(k)	Titled blue cases	125-150

George Petersen

Nr. 119(i)

George Petersen

Verleihungsurkunde

Im Namen des
Oberbefehlshabers der Luftwaffe

verleihe ich dem

Hauptmann Heinrich W o h l e r s

IV./ Nachtjagdgeschwader 4

die

Frontflug-Spange für Nacht-Jäger
in Gold

Gefechtsstand , den 13.Juli 194 3

Oberst und Geschwaderkommodore.

Nr. 119(f)

Verleihungsurkunde

Im Namen des
Oberbefehlshabers der Luftwaffe

verleihe ich dem

Gefreiten Kurt S c h m i d t

7./Nachtjagdgeschwader 1

die

Frontflug-Spange für Nacht-Jäger
in Bronze

Gefechtsstand , den 3. 3. 194 4
m. d. W. d. G. b.

Major

Nr. 119(j)

George Petersen

120. **Luftwaffe Long-Range Day Fighters & Air-to-Ground Support**
Squadrons 1941-44 (Downward Arrow)
(Frontflugspange für Zerstörer und Schlachtflieger)

(a)	Gold Class with Pendant (numbered missions)	$750-1,000
(b)	Certificate	400-500
(c)	Gold Class with Pendant (flower design)	750-850
(d)	Certificate	400
(e)	Gold Class	600-650
(f)	Certificate	350
(g)	Silver Class	400
(h)	Certificate	200-250
(i)	Bronze Class	300
(j)	Certificate	150-200

* Prices apply to only early quality clasps, late war issues
in zinc (crude) would be priced at some 20% less.

(k)	Titled blue cases	150

Nr. 120

121. **Luftwaffe Long Range Night Fighter & Night Intruder Squadrons**
Clasp 1941-45 (Downward Arrow)
(Frontflugspange Fernnachtjäger)

(a)	Gold Class with Pendant (numbered missions)	$750-1,000
(b)	Certificate	500-600
(c)	Gold Class with Pendant (flower design)	750-850
(d)	Certificate	400
(e)	Gold Class	500
(f)	Certificate	250-300
(g)	Silver Class	500
(h)	Certificate	200-250
(i)	Bronze Class	350
(j)	Certificate	150-200

** Prices apply to only early quality clasps, late war issues
in zinc (crude) would be priced at some 20% less.

(k)	Titled blue cases	125-150

George Petersen

Nr. 121(a)

122. Luftwaffe Heavy/Medium & Dive Bombers Squadron Clasp (Frontflugspange für Kampfflieger)

(a)	Gold Class with Pendant (numbered missions)	$450-550
(b)	Certificate	200-250
(c)	Gold Class with Pendant (flower design)	400-450
(d)	Certificate	200
(e)	Gold Class	300
(f)	Certificate	150-175
(g)	Silver Class	200
(h)	Certificate	125
(i)	Bronze Class	100
(j)	Certificate	80

** Prices apply to only early quality clasp, late war issues
in zinc (crude) would be priced at some 30% less.

(k)	Case	75

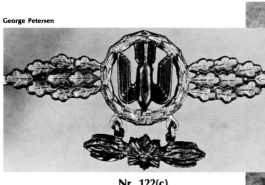

Nr. 122(c)

Oberfeldwebel Walter Pilz wears the Bomber's
Clasp with Pendant.

Frontflugspange
für Kampfflieger
filber

Nr. 122(k)

123. Luftwaffe Reconnaissance, Air/Sea Rescue & Meteorological Clasp (Frontflungspange für Aufklärer)

(a)	Gold Class with Pendant (numbered missions)	$500-600
(b)	Certificate	250-300
(c)	Gold Class with Pendant (flower design)	450-500
(d)	Certificate	250
(e)	Gold Class	350
(f)	Certificate	200
(g)	Silver Class	250
(h)	Certificate	150
(i)	Bronze Class	150
(j)	Certificate	100

** Prices apply to only early quality clasp, late war issues
in zinc (crude) would be priced at some 30% less.

(k)	Titled blue cases	90

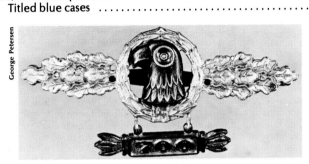

George Petersen

Nr. 123(a)

George Petersen

Derleihungsurkunde

Im Namen des
Oberbefehlshabers der Luftwaffe

verleihe ich dem

Oberfeldwebel Albert S c h ü m a c h e r,

Aufkl. Staffel 1.(F)/33

die

Frontflug-Spange für Aufklärer

in Silber

O.U. , den 28. 8. 1942

Oberstleutnant und Kommandeur
Aufklärungsgruppe 123.

Nr. 123(h)

Nr. 123(k)

124. **Luftwaffe Transport & Glider Squadron Clasp**
     (Frontflugspange für Transportflieger)

(a)	Gold Class with Pendant (numbered missions)	$500-600
(b)	Certificate	250-300
(c)	Gold Class with Pendant (flower design)	450-500
(d)	Certificate	250
(e)	Gold Class	350
(f)	Certificate	200
(g)	Silver Class	250
(h)	Certificate	150
(i)	Bronze Class	150
(j)	Certificate	100

** Prices apply to only early quality clasps, late war issues
in zinc (crude) would be priced at some 30% less.

(k)	Titled blue cases	100

Verleihungsurkunde

Im Namen des
Oberbefehlshabers der Luftwaffe

verleihe ich dem

Unteroffizier Karl Heinz P r a h m,

3./Kampfgruppe z.b.V.106

die

Frontflug-Spange für Transportflieger

in Bronze

O.U., den 20.6. 19_2

Oberstlt.u.Kommandeur

Nr. 124(j)

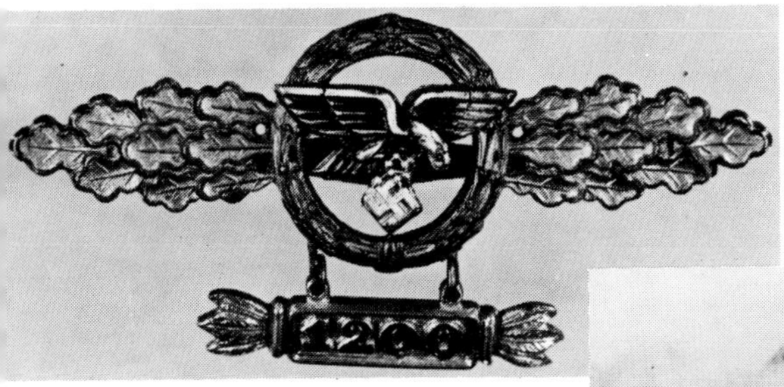

George Petersen

Nr. 124(a)

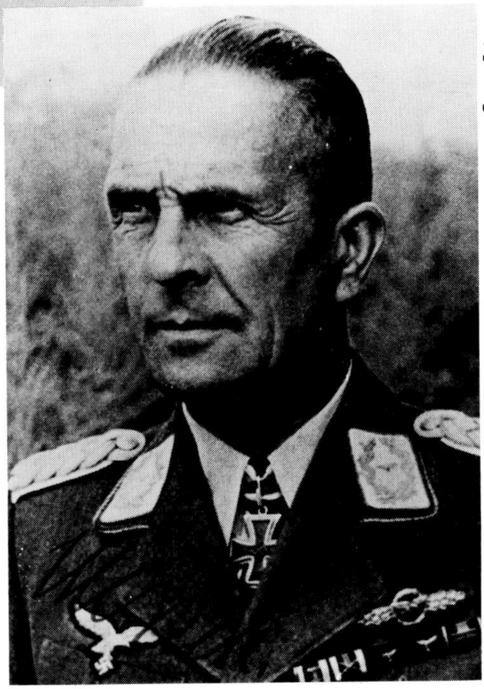

George Petersen

Generalmajor Friedrich Morzik wearing the Transport Clasp.

125. Luftwaffe Air-to-Ground Support Squadrons Clasp 1944-45 (Frontflugspange für Schlachtflieger)

(a)	Gold Class with Pendant (numbered missions)	$650-850
(b)	Certificate	400-450
(c)	Gold Class	600-700
(d)	Certificate	400
(e)	Silver Class	400
(f)	Certificate	200-250
(g)	Bronze Class	300
(h)	Certificate	150-200

** Prices apply to only early quality clasps, late war issues in zinc (crude) would be priced at some 20% less.

(i)	Titled blue cases	150

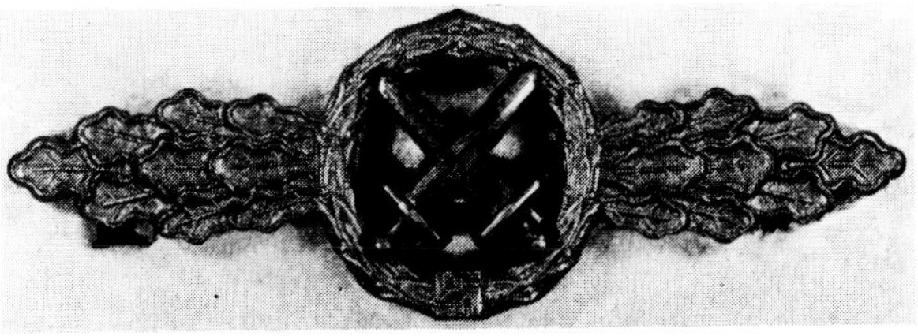

George Petersen

Nr. 125

Verleihungsurkunde

Im Namen des
Oberbefehlshabers der Luftwaffe

verleihe ich dem

Obergefreiten Josef Nieporte,

3./Nachtschlachtgruppe 2,

die

Frontflug=Spange für Schlachtflieger

in Bronze

O. U. , den 21. 10. 1944

Major und Gruppenkommandeur

Nr. 125(h)

Luftwaffe personnel utilized bullion versions of the Frontflugspange. To date, the only variations observed are as follows:

Fighter Clasp \$300
Bomber Clasp 300
Reconnaissance Clasp 300

George Petersen

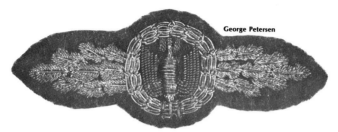

Nr. 122 (bullion)

George Petersen

Reconnaissance pilot and Knight's Cross Holder, Oblt. Martin Meisel, wears a bullion version of the Reconnaissance Clasp and Iron Cross 1st Class.

126. Luftwaffe Goblet of Honor - for outstanding achievement in the air 1940-45 (Ehrenpokal für Besondere Leistung im Luftkrieg)

(a)	1st type in hallmarked "800" silver by "Wagner"	$2,000*
(b)	2nd type in alpaka silverplate by "Wagner"	1,500
(c)	Certificate	600
(d)	1st type red leather shaped case	750
(e)	2nd type blue leatherette box-case	600

*If named to a Knight's Cross holder the value can be significantly higher.

D. Littlejohn

Nr. 126

Ich verleihe
dem

Gefreiten
Walter G o l e t z
in Anerkennung seiner hervorragenden Tapferkeit
und der besonderen Erfolge als Schlachtflieger

den Ehrenpokal
für besondere Leistung
im Luftkrieg

Hauptquartier des Ob. d. L., den 21. Juni 1944

Der Reichsminister der Luftfahrt
und Oberbefehlshaber der Luftwaffe

Göring.

Reichsmarschall

Die erfolgte Verleihung wird beglaubigt:
Der Chef des Luftwaffenpersonalamts

Generaloberst

Nr. 126(c)

The Goblet of Honor is shown being awarded to these three Luftwaffe NCO's.

107

G. Del Collo

Goblet of Honor (Nr. 126) and red leather case (Nr. 126(d)).

Ich verleihe
dem

Feldwebel
Hans G u n t e r m a n n
in Anerkennung seiner hervorragenden Tapferkeit
beim Kampf um die Insel Leros

die Ehrenschale
für hervorragende
Kampfleistungen

Hauptquartier des Ob. d. L., den 29. September 1944

Der Reichsminister der Luftfahrt
und Oberbefehlshaber der Luftwaffe

Göring

Reichsmarschall

Die erfolgte Verleihung wird beglaubigt:
Der Chef des Luftwaffenpersonalamts

Generaloberst

Nr. 127(b)

127. Luftwaffe Salver of Honor - for distinguished achiements
   in action 1942-45
   (Ehrenschale für Hervorragende Kampfleistungen)
(a)   Fine quality alpaka silverplate by "Wagner" $4,500
(b)   Certificate 1,500
(c)   Case 750-1,000
** Always engraved with recipient's name, rank, and date.

Nr. 127

128. Luftwaffe Silvered Large Medallion for Outstanding Achievements
   in the Technical Branch of the Air Force
   (Medaille für Ausgezeichnete Leistungen im Technischen
   Dienst der Luftwaffe)
(a)   Medallion, 75mm, silverplated $200
(b)   Black case 100

Nr. 128
(obverse)

Nr. 128
(reverse)

129. **Luftwaffe Air District West France Medallion for Meritorious Achievements (Feldluftgaukommando Westfrankreich Luftgauplakette für Treue Dienstleistungen)**

(a)	Bronze, 41mm	$250
(b)	Miniature (half size) lapel badge, 20mm	150
(c)	Certificate	250

Nr. 129 (obverse)   Nr. 129 (reverse)

130. Luftwaffe Air District Belgium-Northern France Medallion for Meritorious Achievements (Luftgaukommando Belgien Nordfankreich Luftgauplakette für Treue Dienstleistungen)
(a)   Bronze, 41mm $250
(b)   Certificate 250

Nr. 130 (obverse)   Nr. 130 (reverse)

131. Luftwaffe Plaque for Outstanding Achievement & Merit in the 21st Air Force Field Division 1942 (Plakette für Hervorragende Leistungen und Verdienste im 21. Luftwaffen Felddivision)
(a)   Cast iron plaque $300
(b)   Certificate 250

132. Luftwaffe Plaque for Special Achievement in the Air District Norway (Plakette für Besondere Leistung im Luftgau Norwegen)
(a)   Bronzed color, cast iron (local manufacture) $200-250
(b)   Certificate 250

Nr. 131

Nr. 132

George Petersen

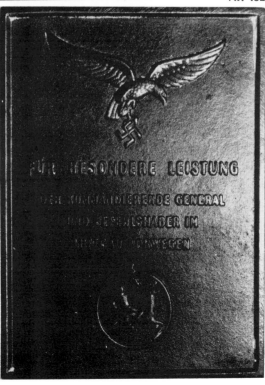

(Above) A variant pattern Luftwaffe plaque for Special Achievement in Air District Norway.

113

Ich überreiche dem

Obergefreiten

F r i t s c h e (Rolf)

den Ehrenschild des Luftgaukomman-
dos mit meiner dankbaren Anerken-
nung für die in Norwegen geleisteten
Dienste.

Der Kommandierende General und
Befehlshaber im Luftgau Norwegen
m.d.W.d.G.b.

Generalleutnant

O.U., den 5. Januar 1942

Der Ehrenschild hat die Nr. 1420

Certificate for the Air District Norway Plaque.

133/I. **Luftwaffe Plaque for the Southeast Command of the Air Force**
(Luftwaffenkommando Südost Plakette)

(a) $300
(b) Certificate 250

133/II. **Luftwaffe Plaque for Outstanding Technical Achievements in the Southern**
Command
(Plakette für Hervoragende Technische Leistungen im Süden)

(a) Cast iron plaque $200-250
(b) Certificate 250

Nr. 133/I   Nr. 133/II

134. Luftwaffe G.O.C. Air District Staff Finland's Plaque for Proof of Merit 1943
(Der Kommandierende General des Luftgau-Stabes Finnland für Besondere Bewährung)

(a)   Bronze plaque (reverse numbered) $250
(b)   Certificate 250

Nr. 134

Für Besondere Bewährung

verleihe ich dem

Oberst

Hans A r p s

Luftgaustab Finnland

die Ehrenplakette des Luftgaustabes

Finnland

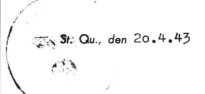

St. Qu., den 20.4.43

Der Kommandierende General
des Luftgaustabes Finnland

~~General der Flieger~~

Oberst i.G.

Certificate for the Air District Staff Finland Plaque.

135. **Luftwaffe Plaque for Outstanding Achievement in Air District XI**
   (Plakette für Hervorragende Leistung im Luftgau XI)

(a)   1st Type - cast bronze $300

(b)   2nd Type - bronzed metal, Bronze Class 250

(c)   2nd Type - silvered metal - Silver Class 250

               *   Engraved with recipient's name and rank.

(d)   Certificate 250

Nr. 135(a)

Nr. 135(a),
variant

Nr. 135(b)

NOTE:
It should be noted that variations exist of both the 1st and 2nd
Type of Luftgau XI.

Als
Anerkennung
für hervorragende Leistung

überreiche ich
Oberst

von H i p p e l
Kdr. der 3.Flakdivision
den

Eisernen Ehrenschild
des Luftgaues XI

Der Kommandierende General
und Befehlshaber im Luftgau XI

General der Flieger

Hamburg, den 24.Dezember 194 2

Certificate for iron/bronze class of the Air District XI Plaque.

Certificate for silver class of the Air District XI Plaque.

Als
Anerkennung
für hervorragende Leistung

überreiche ich

Generalmajor von H i p p e l
Kdr. 3. Flakdivision

den

Silbernen Ehrenschild
des Luftgaues XI

Der Kommandierende General
und Befehlshaber im Luftgau XI

General der Flieger

Hamburg, den 24. Dezember 194 2

**136. Luftwaffe Plaque in Recognition of Special Merit in
The Battle of Crete 1941
(Plakette in Anerkennung Besonderer Verdienste im Einsatz Kreta)**

(a)   Bronze plaque (velvet backed) $450

         * Engraved with recipient's name and rank.

(b)   Certificate 300

Nr. 136(a)

137. Armed Forces Long Service Award
(Wehrmacht-Dienstauszeichnungen)

(a)	Silver Medal for 4 years	$30
(b)	Certificate	30-40
(c)	Gold Medal for 12 years	45
(d)	Certificate	40-50
(e)	Silver Cross for 18 years	100
(f)	Certificate	65-75
(g)	Gold Cross for 25 years	125
(h)	Certificate	85-100
(i)	Gold Cross & Oakleaf Emblem for 40 years	250
(j)	Certificate	200
(k)	Paper packets for 4 & 12 year medals	20
(l)	Green carton for 18 year cross	30
(m)	Green case for 25 and 40 year crosses	60

** All above applies only to awards complete with Eagle-emblems on original ribbons.

Nr's. 137(a) & (c)

Nr. 137(a)
(reverse)

Nr. 137(c)
(reverse)

Nr. 137(e)

Nr. 137(e)
(reverse)

Im Namen des Führers und Reichskanzlers

verleihe ich dem

Hauptmann Friedrich Karl Großenbrücker
(Dienstgrad, Vor- und Zuname)

Luftgaukommando XIII
(Truppenteil)

für   4   jährige treue Dienste in der Wehrmacht

Dienstauszeichnung   IV.   Klasse.

Nürnberg   , den 18. Juli 19 39

Der Kommandeur im Luftgau XIII

i. v.

O b e r s t

Nr. 137(b)

Nr's. 137(g) & (i)
(reverse)

Nr. 137(i)

Nr. 137(i)

George Petersen

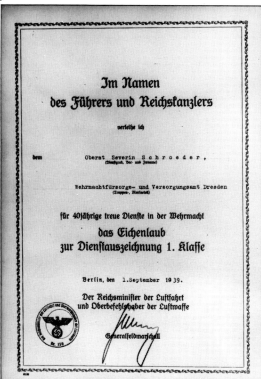

Im Namen
des Führers und Reichskanzlers

verleihe ich

dem   Oberst Severin S c h r o e d e r ,
                    (Dienstgrad, Vor- und Zuname)

Wehrmachtfürsorge- und Versorgungsamt Dresden
                    (Truppen-, Marineteil)

für 40jährige treue Dienste in der Wehrmacht

das Eichenlaub
zur Dienstauszeichnung 1. Klasse

Berlin, den 1.September 1939.

Der Reichsminister der Luftfahrt
und Oberbefehlshaber der Luftwaffe

Generalfeldmarschall

Nr. 137(j)

123

POLITICAL AND CIVIL
ORDERS, DECORATIONS AND MEDALS
1933-1945

138. **Meritorious Order of the German Eagle 1937-45**
(Verdienstorden vom deutschen Adler)

Grand Cross Sash Cross & 8-pointed Breast Star Set 1937-43

(a) Grosskreuz des deutschen Adlerordens) $5,000
(b) Document in folder 2,000
(c) As above set but with Swords, 1939-43 (mit Schwertern) 6,000
(d) Document in folder 2,500
(e) Large red leather titled case 1,000

Nr's. 138(a), 146(a),
147(a) & 148(a)

Nr's. 138(a), 146(a), 147(a) & 148(a)

Nr's. 138(c), 146(c), 147(c) & 148(c)

Nr's. 138(c), 146(c),
147(c) & 148(c)

139. **Special Class Golden Grand Cross Set 1939**
      (Sonderstufe)

(a)   Grand Cross Set .... *
(b)   Presentation document in folder .... *
(c)   Large red leather titled case .... *
           * **Approximately 16 awarded**

Nr. 139 (gold)

140. Unique Special Grade of Grand Cross Set with Diamonds 1937
   (Sonderstufe mit Brillanten)

(a)   Awarded to Mussolini by Hitler on his State Visit in 1937 . . . .   *
(b)   Presentation document in folder . . . .   *
(c)   Large red leather titled case . . . .   *

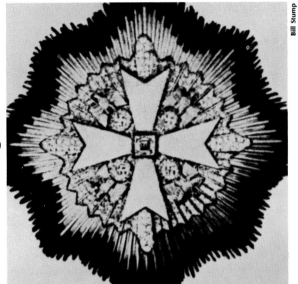

Nr. 140

Bill Stump

Mussolini wears his "Grand Cross of the German Eagle Order in Gold with Diamonds" (Nr. 140) during Hitler's state visit to Italy in May 1938.

127

141. Order of the German Eagle with Star 1937-39
   (Deutsche Adlerorder, mit Stern)

(a)	Neck Cross (50mm) & 6-pointed Breast Star (75mm)	$3,500
(b)	Document in folder	1,500
(c)	Large red leather titled case	600
(d)	As above but with Swords (mit Schwertern)	4,000
(e)	Document in folder	1,500
(f)	Large red leather titled case	600

D. Littlejohn

Nr's. 141(a), 142(a), 149(a) & 150(a)

Nr's. 141(d), 142(c),
149(c) & 150(c)

Nr's. 141(a) & 149(a)

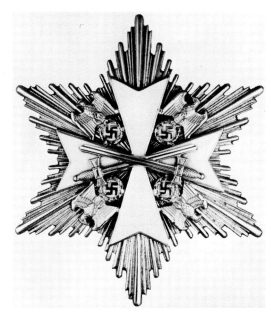

Nr's. 141(d)
& 149(c)

142. Order of the German Eagle 1st Class Neck Cross 1937-43
(Deutsche Adlerorder, Erste Stufe)

(a)	Neck Cross (50mm)	$1,400
(b)	Document in folder	500
(c)	As above but with Swords (mit Schwertern)	1,600
(d)	Document in folder	500
(e)	Large red leather titled case	400

143. Order of the German Eagle, 2nd Class, Pin-back Breast Cross 1937-43
(Deutsche Adlerorder, Zweiter Stufe)

(a)	Pin-back Cross (50mm)	$1,100
(b)	Document in folder	450
(c)	As above but with Swords (mit Schwertern)	1,200
(d)	Document in folder	450
(e)	Small red leather titled case	350

Nr's. 143(a) & 151(a)   Nr's. 143(c) & 151(c)

144. **Order of the German Eagle, 3rd Class, Breast Cross 1937-43**
(Deutsche Adlerorden, Dritte Stufe)

(a)	Breast Cross (45mm)	$900
(b)	Document in folder	400
(c)	As above but with Swords (mit Schwertern)	1,000
(d)	Document in folder	400
(e)	Small red leather titled case	350

Nr. 144(a)

145. **Order of the German Eagle, Medal of Merit in Silver 1937-45**
(Deutsche Verdienst Medaille)

(a)	1st type silver medal 1937-43 (Gothic script)	$400
(b)	Certificate	300
(c)	As above but with Swords 1939-43 (mit Schwertern)	450
(d)	Certificate	300
(e)	Small red leather titled cases	150
(f)	2nd type silver medal 1943-45 (Latin script)	350
(g)	Certificate	250
(h)	As above but with Swords 1943-45 (mit Schwertern)	400
(i)	Certificate 2	250
(j)	2nd type bronze medal 1943-45 (Latin script)	200
(k)	Certificate	150
(l)	2nd type bronze medal with Swords (mit Schwertern)	250
(m)	Certificate	150
(n)	Titled paper packets	100

146. **Grand Cross of the Order of the German Eagle in Gold 1943-45**
(Goldenes Grosskreuz des Deutschen Adlerordens)

(a)	Sash Cross (66mm) & 8-pointed Breast Star (90mm)	*
(b)	Presentation document in folder	*
(c)	As above but with Swords (mit Schwertern)	*
(d)	Presentation document in folder	*
(e)	Large red leather titled case	*

147. **Grand Cross of the Order of the German Eagle 1943-45**
(Grosskreuz des Deutschen Adlerordens)

(a)	Sash Cross (60mm) & 8-pointed Breast Star (80mm)	$4,500
(b)	Document in folder	1,500
(c)	As above but with Swords (mit Schwertern)	5,000
(d)	Document in folder	2,000
(e)	Large red leather titled case	1,000

Nr's. 145(c)
& 145(h)

Nr's. 145(a) &
145(c) (reverse)

148. Order of the German Eagle 1st Class Set 1943-45
(Deutsche Adlerorden Erste Klasse)

(a)	Sash Cross (50mm) & 8-pointed Breast Star (80mm)	$4,000
(b)	Document in folder	1,200
(c)	As above but with Swords (mit Schwertern)	4,500
(d)	Document in folder	1,200
(e)	Large red leather titled case	800

149. Order of the German Eagle 2nd Class Set 1943-45
(Deutsche Adlerorden Zweite Klasse)

(a)	Neck Cross (50mm) & 6-pointed Breast Star (75mm)	$3,000
(b)	Document in folder	800
(c)	As above but with Swords (mit Schwertern)	3,500
(d)	Document in folder	800
(e)	Large red leather titled case	600

150. **Order of the German Eagle 3rd Class 1943-45**
    (Deutsche Adlerorden Dritte Klasse)
(a)   Neck Cross (50mm) $1,200
(b)   Document in folder   500
(c)   As Above but with Swords (mit Schwertern) 1,500
(d)   Document in folder   500
(e)   Large red leather titled case   500

151. **Order of the German Eagle 4th Class 1943-45**
    (Deutsche Adlerorden Vierte Klasse)
(a)   Breast Cross, pin back (50mm) $700
(b)   Document in folder   400
(c)   As above but with Swords (mit Schwertern)   800
(d)   Document in folder   400
(e)   Small red leather titled case   300

152. **Order of the German Eagle 5th Class 1943-45**
    (Deutsche Adlerorden Fünfte Klasse)
(a)   Breast Cross (45mm) worn on ribbon $500
(b)   Document in folder   300
(c)   As above but with Swords (mit Schwertern)   550
(d)   Document in folder   300
(e)   Small red leather titled case   250

Nr. 152(c)

153. The German Order 1942-45
(Deutscher Orden)

(a)	Neck Cross with oak leaves and swords (Halskreuz)	$7,500
(b)	Presentation document in folder	10,000
(c)	As above but without oak leaves and swords	6,000
(d)	Presentation document in folder	7,500
(e)	Breast Cross, pin back (Steckkreuz)	6,000
(f)	Presentation document in folder	7,500
(g)	Red leather titled case	1,500

Nr. 153(a)

Nr. 153(c)

Nr. 153(e)

133

154. **German National Prize for Art & Science 1937-45**
     (Ehrenzeichen des Deutschen Nationalpreises für
     Kunst und Wissenschaft)
(a)   Massive Breast Star, pin back in gold platinum,
          inset with diamond brilliants $30,000
(b)   Silk sash and rosette complete with plaque 10,000
(c)   Large presentation document in folder 25,000
(d)   Large presentation case   5,000

O. Spronk

Nr. 154

155. **German Red Cross Decorations 1934-37 (No Swastika)**
     (Ehrenzeichen der Deutschen Roten Kreuzes)
(a)   1st Class Neck Cross (53mm) (Erste Klasse) $450
(b)   Certificate   200
(c)   Breast Star (73mm) pin back (stern) 1,000
(d)   Certificate   350
(e)   Cross of Merit, pin back (Verdienstkreuz)   150
(f)   Certificate   100
(g)   Decoration of the Red Cross (40mm) on
          breast ribbon (Ehrenzeichen)   75
(h)   Certificate   50
(i)   Ladies Cross (40mm) worn on ribbon bow (Damenkreuz).........   75
(j)   Certificate   50
(k)   Red leather titled cases 50-100

134

Nr. 155(a)

Nr. 155(c)

Mit Zustimmung des Führers und Reichskanzlers

Adolf Hitler

verleihe ich als Zeichen der Dankbarkeit
und in Anerkennung für besondere Dienste

Herrn Commander Murphy

das Verdienstkreuz

des Ehrenzeichens des Deutschen Roten Kreuzes

Berlin, den
13. Jan 1938

Carl Eduard

Herzog von Sachsen-Coburg und Gotha

Präsident des Deutschen Roten Kreuzes

✠

Mit Zustimmung des Führers und Reichskanzlers

Adolf Hitler

verleihe ich als Zeichen der Dankbarkeit
und in Anerkennung für besondere Dienste

Herrn Stabsarzt
Dr. med. Heinrich Neumann

die Zweite Klasse

des Ehrenzeichens des Deutschen Roten Kreuzes

Berlin, den
9. Nov. 1934

Carl Eduard

Herzog von Sachsen-Coburg und Gotha

Präsident des Deutschen Roten Kreuzes

Nr. 155(e)

Nr. 155(g), illus-
trated is the 1922-
1934 pattern.

Nr. 155(g)

Nr. 155(i), illustrated
is the 1922-1934 pattern

156. German Red Cross Decorations 1937-39 (With Swastika) (Ehrenzeichen des Deutschen Roten Kreuzes)

(a)	Grand Cross Sash Badge (52mm) & Breast Star (84mm) (Grosskreuz)	$4,500
(b)	Document in folder	600
(c)	Breast Star (84mm) (Stern)	2,500
(d)	Document in folder	600
(e)	1st Class Neck Cross with Oak Leaves (52mm) (Erste Stufe)	1,200
(f)	Document in folder	500
	Special Grade Neck Cross with Diamonds (Sonderstufe mit Brillanten)	*
(h)	Special presentation document in folder	*
(i)	Cross of Merit (Verdienstkreuz) pin back	400
(j)	Certificate	200
(k)	2nd Class Breast Cross (Zweite Klasse) worn on ribbon	150
(l)	Certificate	75
(m)	Women's Cross (Frauenkreuz) worn on ribbon bow	150
(n)	Certificate	75
(o)	Enamelled Medal (Medaille)	125
(p)	Certificate	60
	Red leatherette cases for all above classes of decoration	

** Prices are for cased pieces

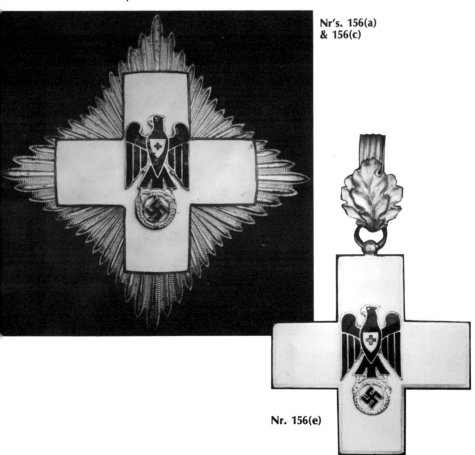

Nr's. 156(a)
& 156(c)

Nr. 156(e)

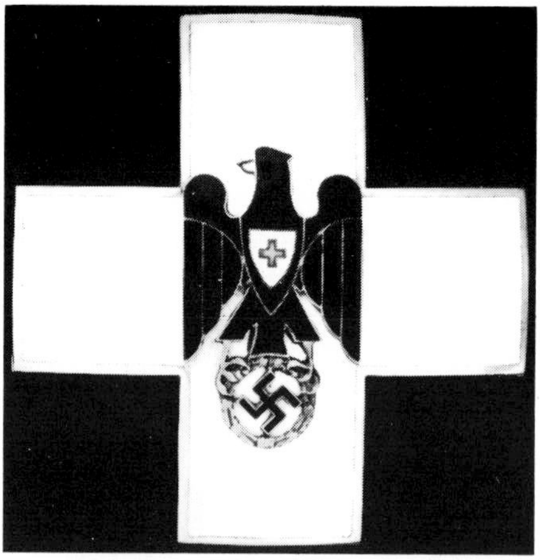

Nr. 156(i)

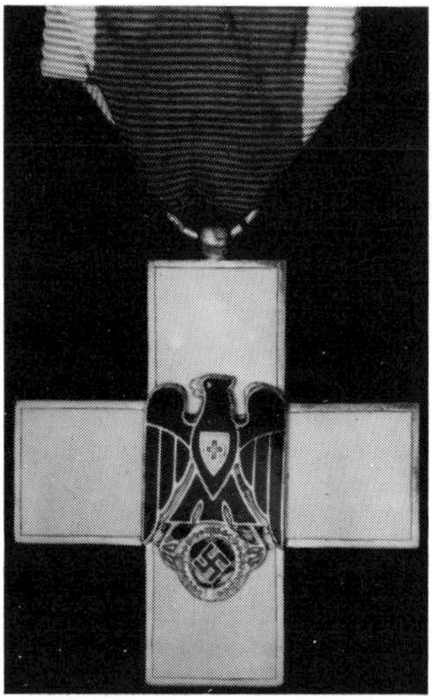

Nr. 156(k)

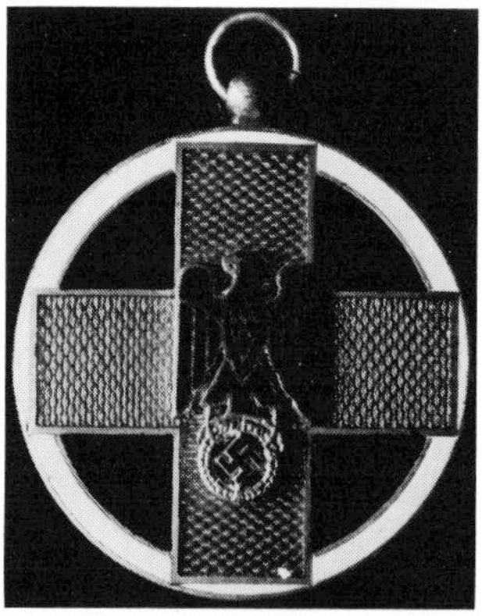

Nr. 156(o)

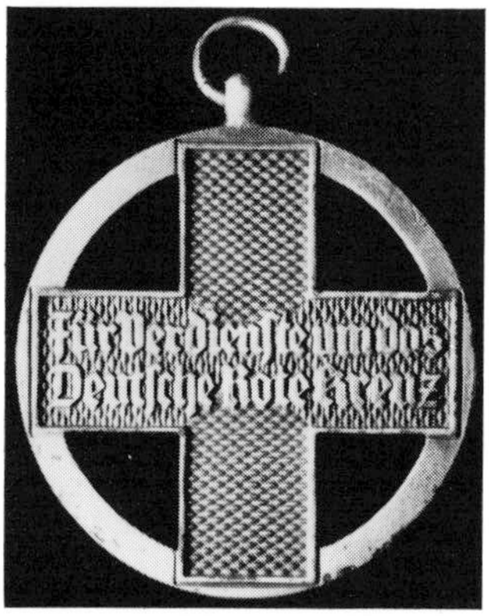
Für Verdienste um das
Deutsche Rote Kreuz

Nr. 156(o) (reverse)

157. D.R.K. Sister's Cross
   (Das D.R.K. Schwesternkreuz)

(a)	Silver Cross for 10 years	$200
(b)	Certificate	100
(c)	Silver Cross for 25 years	300
(d)	Certificate	100
(e)	D.R.K. Long Service Cross for Matron (Oberin) (Gold)	400
(f)	Certificate	150
(g)	D.R.K. Long Service Cross for Senior Matron (Gen.Oberin) (Gold)	600
(h)	Certificate	200

Nr's. 157(a) & 157(c)   Nr's. 157(e) & 157(g)

158. D.R.K. Pin of Honor
   (Ehrennadel des D.R.K.)

(a)	Pin	$150
(b)	Certificate	100

Nr. 158

159. German Social Welfare Decorations (1939-45)
   (Ehrenzeichen für Deutsche Volkspflege)

(a)	Special Class Sash Badge (52mm) & Breast Star (84mm) (Sonderstufe)	*
(b)	Document in folder	*

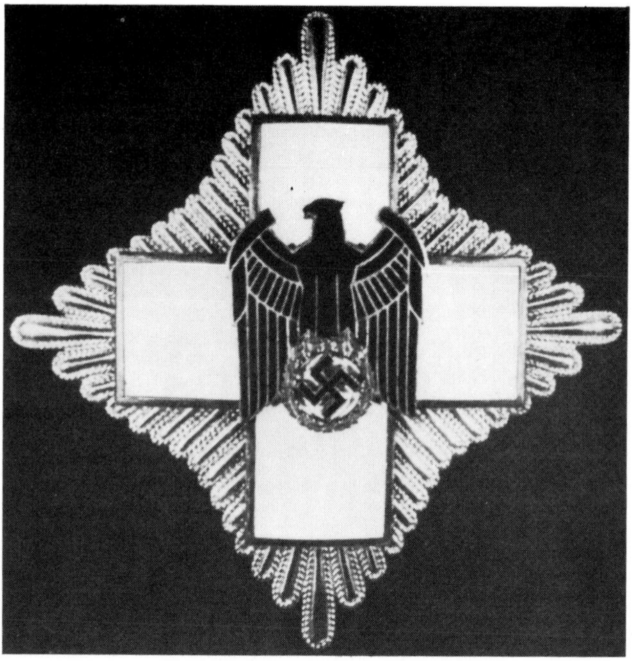

Nr. 159(a)

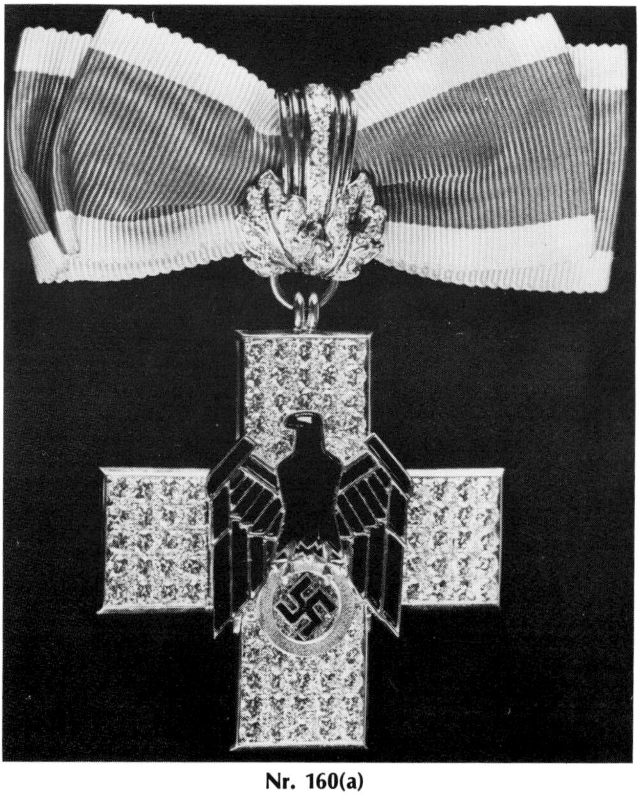

Nr. 160(a)

160. German Social Welfare Decorations
(Ehrenzeichen für Deutsche Volkspflege)

(a)   Special Class 1st Class Ladies' Decoration with diamonds . . . .   *

(b)   Special presentation document in folder . . . .   *

(c)   Special presentation casket . . . .   *

           Above awarded to ladies only on ribbon bow

(d)   1st Class Neck Cross (52mm) (Erste Stufe) $1,250

(e)   Certificate 400

(f)   2nd Class Breast Cross pin back (Zweite Stufe) 350

(g)   Certificate 200

(h)   3rd Class Breast Cross on ribbon (Dritte Stufe) 125

(i)   Certificate 100

(j)   Social Welfare Medal (Medaille) 30

(k)   Certificate 30

(l)   Red leatherette cases for all classes of decorations, except
           medal which has titled paper packet 75-250

Nr. 160(f)

Nr. 160(d)

Note:
Above prices are for
cased pieces.

Nr. 160(h)

Nr. 160(j)   Nr. 160(j) (reverse)

161. German Olympic Games Decorations 1936
   (Deutschen Olympiaehrenzeichen)

(a)   1st Class Neck Cross (Erste Stufe) $1,500
(b)   Certificate 600
(c)   2nd Class Breast Cross (Zweite Stufe) 500
(d)   Certificate 300
(e)   White leatherette cases for above decorations 150-250

Nr. 161(a)

Nr. 161(c)

In Anerkennung seiner Verdienste
um die Deutschland übertragenen
Olympischen Spiele 1936
verleihe ich dem

SS.-Brigadeführer Karl Wolff

das

Deutsche Olympia-Ehrenzeichen
erster Klasse.

Berlin, den *12. Oktober* 1936

Der Führer und Reichskanzler

Nr. 161(b)

162. Olympic Games Commemorative Medal 1936
(Olympia-Erinnerungsmedaille)
(a) Medal $90-125
(b) Certificate 125
(c) White leatherette case 50

Nr. 162

Nr. 162
(reverse)

163. Civil Defense Decorations 1938
   (Luftschutz Ehrenzeichen)

(a)	1st Class Cross (Erste Stufe)	$300-400
(b)	Certificate	150
(c)	Grey case	60
(d)	2nd Class Medal (Zweite Stufe)	30
(e)	Certificate	25
(f)	Either grey carton or titled paper packet	35-50

Nr. 163(a)

Nr. 163(a) (reverse)

Nr. 163(e)

DER FÜHRER
HAT MIT ERLASS VOM HEUTIGEN TAGE

dem Fahrer im Werkluftschutz

Emil H e n n i n g e r

in Mannheim

IN ANERKENNUNG
SEINER VERDIENSTE IM LUFTSCHUTZ
DAS
LUFTSCHUTZ-EHRENZEICHEN
ZWEITER STUFE
VERLIEHEN.

BERLIN, den 30. September 1943

DER STAATSMINISTER UND CHEF
DER PRÄSIDIALKANZLEI

Nr. 163(d)   Nr. 163(d) (reverse)

164. Fire Brigade Decorations 1936
(Feuerwehr Ehrenzeichen)

(a)	1st Class Cross (60mm) 1936, pin back (Erste Stufe)	$750
(b)	Certificate	300
(c)	1st Class Cross (43mm) 1938, pin back (Erste Stufe)	500
(d)	Certificate	150
(e)	2nd Class Cross (33mm) on breast ribbon (Zweite Stufe)	125
(f)	Certificate	75
(g)	Large titled paper packet for 1st Class 1936 (60mm) Cross	75
(h)	Black leatherette cases for other crosses	50

Nr's. 164(a) & 164(c)

Nr. 164(e)

165. Mine Rescue Service Decorations 1936
(Grubenwehr-Ehrenzenchen)

(a)	Large pin back Medal 1936 (50mm)	$750
(b)	Certificate	250
(c)	Silver Medal 1938 (35mm)	150
(d)	Certificate	100
(e)	Black leatherette cases for both medals	50

Nr. 165(a)

Nr. 165(c)

Nr. 165(c)
(reverse)

166. **Cross of Honor of the German Mother 1938**
      (Ehrenzeichen der Deutschen Mutter)

(a)	1st Class in Gold "Das Kind Adelt die Mutter" 1938	$1,000
(b)	Certificate	150
(c)	2nd Class in Silver "Das Kind Adelt die Mutter" 1938	750
(d)	Certificate	100
(e)	3rd Class in Bronze "Das Kind Adelt die Mutter" 1938	600
(f)	Certificate	100
(g)	1st Class in Gold (16 Dezember 1938)	40
(h)	Certificate	60
(i)	2nd Class in Silver (16 Dezember 1938)	30
(j)	Certificate	40
(k)	3rd Class in Bronze (16 Dezember 1938)	20
(l)	Certificate	30
(m)	1st Class blue case	50
(n)	2nd & 3rd Classes in large titled paper packets	30

Nr's. 166(a),
166(c), 166(e),
166(g), 166(i)
& 166(k)

Nr's. 166(a),
166(c) & 166(e)

Jm Namen
des
Deutſchen Volkes
verleihe ich

die erſte Stufe
des
Ehrenkreuzes
der Deutſchen Mutter

Berlin, den 1. Oktober 1939

Der Führer

Nr. 166(h)

**167. German Life Saving Medal 1937
(Rettungsmedaille)**

(a)	Type A	Official issue by Prussian State Mint in "800" hallmarked silver (silber)	$250
(b)	Type B	Private purchase silver-plated brass or metal	100
(c)		Certificate	350
(d)		Black leatherette case	60

Nr. 167(a)
(reverse)

Nr. 167(a)

168. German Life Saving Medallion 1937
(Erinnerungs Medaille für Rettung aus Gefahr)

(a)   Fine quality silver striking (48mm) $300

(b)   Certificate 300

(c)   Black leatherette case 50

Nr. 168   Nr. 168 (reverse)

169. Eagle Shield of Germany 1934
(Adlerschild des Deutschen Reiches)

(a)   Large bronze medallion (110mm) .... *

(b)   Certificate .... *

(c)   Case .... *

Nr. 169

170. Goethe Medal for Art & Science 1933
(Goethe Medaille für Kunst und Wissenschaft)

(a)   Large silver medallion (71mm) .... *
(b)   Certificate .... *
(c)   Case .... *

Nr. 170

Im Namen
des
Deutschen Volkes

verleihe ich

die von dem verewigten
Herrn Reichspräsidenten von Hindenburg
gestiftete

Goethe-Medaille
für Kunst und Wissenschaft

den

Der führer und Reichskanzler

Nr. 170 (reverse)

Nr. 170(b)

171. Badge of Honor for Members of the National Senate of Culture 1936
   (Ehrenplakette für die Mitglieder des Reichskultursenats)
(a)   Badge hallmarked silver gilt and enamel
         numbered on reverse $3,000
(b)   Case 400

Nr. 171

172. German Academy for Aeronautical Research Membership Badge 1938
   (Die Deutsche Akademie der Luftfahrforschung)
(a)   President's chain of office (Amtskette)
         hallmarked silver gilt $15,000
(b)   Gold Badge for Honorary Members (57mm) 3,000
(c)   Silver Badge for Sponsoring Members
         (Forderden Mitgliedern) (57mm) 2,500
(d)   Bronze Badge for Corresponding Members
         (Korrespondierenden Mitgliedern) 2,000
(e)   Miniature Badges for Gilt, Silver & Bronze Classes 750
(f)   Black leatherette cases for badges (57mm) 400

Nr's. 172(b), 172(c) & 172(d)

Nr. 172(a)

173. **"Pioneer of Labor" Decoration 1940**
(Ehrenzeichen "Pionier der Arbeit")

(a)	Gilt & enamel (riveted) pin pack	$2,000
(b)	Large presentation document	3,000
(c)	Large red case	500

Nr. 173

174. Badge of Honor of the Dr. Fritz Todt Prize
(Ehrennadel des Dr. Fritz Todt-Preises)

Type A Actual award badges with date "8.2.44." on reverse
(a)	1st Class in Gold (Erste Stufe)	$2,500
(b)	Presentation document	3,000
(c)	2nd Class in Silver (Zweite Stufe)	1,000
(d)	Certificate	750
(e)	3rd Class in Steel (Dritte Stufe)	750
(f)	Certificate	300
(g)	Black leatherette cases	150

Type B* Private purchase badges with plain reverses
(h)	1st Class in Gold (Erste Stufe)	750
(i)	2nd Class in Silver (Zweite Stufe)	350
(j)	3rd Class in Steel (Dritte Stufe)	250

Type C* Variation title "Dr.Ing. Fritz Todt Preis." with plain reverse
(k)	1st Class in Gold (Erste Stufe)	1,500
(l)	2nd Class in Silver (Zweite Stufe)	800
(m)	3rd Class in Steel (Dritte Stufe)	500

* Above examples usually found on manufacturer's sample boards or loose ex-military tailor shops.

Nr's. 174(a), 174(c), 174(e),
174(h), 174(i) & 174(j)

175. "Defense Economy Leader" Decoration 1939
(Ehrenzeichen "Wehrwirtschaftsführer")

(a)	Gilt bronze pin pack	$400
(b)	Miniature half size stock pin badge	150

176. Silver Clasp for Female S.S. Auxiliaries 1943
(Silberspange der S.S. Helferinnen)

(a)	Hallmarked "800" silver pin back (Silber)	$2,500

Nr. 175

Nr. 176

177. S.S. Long Service Awards 1938
(S.S. Dienstauszeichnungen)

(a)	Black medal for 4 years	$125
(b)	Certificate	200
(c)	Carton (black with white S.S./Sigrunes)	90
(d)	Bronze medal for 8 years	200
(e)	Certificate	250
(f)	Carton (black with silver S.S./Sigrunes)	100
(g)	Silver Cross (Swastika) for 12 years	750
(h)	Certificate	350
(i)	Case (black with silver S.S./Sigrunes)	150
(j)	Gold Cross (Swastika) for 25 years	1,000
(k)	Certificate	400
(l)	Case (black with Gold S.S./Sigrunes)	200

Nr. 177(a)

Nr. 177(a) (reverse)

Nr. 177(d)

Nr. 177(d)
(reverse)

Bob Kraus

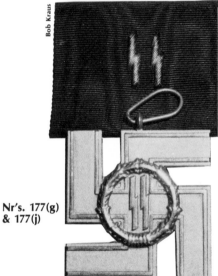

Nr's. 177(g)
& 177(j)

Nr's. 177(g)
& 177(j)
(reverse)

Nr. 177(l)

178. Faithful Service Decorations 1938
(Treudienst Ehrenzeichen)

(a)	Special Class for 50 Years (Sonderstufe)	$150
(b)	Certificate	100
(c)	Case with red "50"	50
(d)	1st Class in Gold for 40 Years (Erste Stufe)	40
(e)	Certificate	50
(f)	Case, red with "40"	20
(g)	2nd Class in Silver for 25 Years (Zweite Stufe)	30
(h)	Certificate	30
(i)	Case, red with "25"	15

Nr. 178(a)

Nr. 178(f)

Jm Namen
des
Deutſchen Volkes
verleihe ich

den Oberpostinspektor
Hermann Schwarz
in Stuttgart

als Anerkennung für 40jährige treue Dienſte
das
goldene
Treudienſt=Ehrenzeichen.

Berlin, den   16. Dezember 1939

Der führer und Reichskanzler

Nr. 178(e)

Nr's. 178(d) &
178(g)

Nr. 178(i)

Nr's. 178(d) &
178(g) (reverse)

179. **Police Expert Skier Badge 1942**
(Polizei Schiführerabzeichen)
Grey aluminum, pin back $850-1,000

Nr. 179

180. Police Expert Alpine & High Alpine Badges 1936
(Gendarmerie Alpine/Hoch-Alpinistabzeichen)
Both Austrian manufacture and style of attachment on reverse.
Silvered brass & enamel with maker's mark $850-1,000

Nr. 180   Nr. 181

181. Police Mountain Guard Badge
(Bergwacht-Hilfspolizei)
Heavy silvered metal, pin back, massive $750

182. Police Bergführer Badge-1941
(Polizei-Bergführer der Ordnungspolizei)
Silvered brass and enamel, pin back $1,000

Nr. 182

183. Police Long Service Awards 1938
(Polizei Dienstauszeichnungen)

(a)   1st Class in Gold for 25 years $150
(b)   Certificate 125
(c)   Case 60
(d)   2nd Class in Silver for 18 years 120
(e)   Certificate 95
(f)   Case 45
(g)   Silver medal for 8 years 65
(h)   Certificate 60
(i)   Carton 30

Nr's. 183(a) & 183(d)   Nr's. 183(a) & 183(d) (reverse)

Nr. 183(g)   Nr. 183(g) (reverse)

184. Customs Service Decoration 1939
(Zollgrenzschutz-Ehrenzeichen)

(a)	Decoration	$125
(b)	Certificate	85
(c)	Case	35

Nr. 184   Nr. 184 (reverse)

185. National Labor Service Long Service Awards 1938 (R.A.D.)
(Dienstauszeichnungen für den Reichsarbeitsdienst)

Type A First design as awarded to male personnel
(a)	1st Class Medal in Gold for 25 years with Eagle Emblem on Ribbon	$200
(b)	Certificate	120
(c)	Case	50
(d)	2nd Class in Silver for 18 years with Silver Eagle Emblem on Ribbon	125
(e)	Certificate	75
(f)	Case	40
(g)	3rd Class Silver Medal for 12 years	60
(h)	Certificate	30
(i)	Carton	15
(j)	4th Class Bronze Medal for 4 years	30
(k)	Certificate	30
(l)	Carton	20

Type B Second design as awarded to female personnel, worn on ribbon bow
(a)	1st Class Medal in Gold for 25 years with Eagle Emblem on ribbon	$300
(b)	Certificate	125
(c)	Case	50
(d)	2nd Class in Silver for 18 years with Silver Eagle Emblem on ribbon	$200
(e)	Certificate	75
(f)	Case	40
(g)	3rd Class Silver Medal for 12 years	150
(h)	Certificate	60
(i)	Carton	40
(j)	4th Class Bronze Medal for 4 years	100
(k)	Certificate	50
(l)	Carton	40

Nr's. 185(a),
185(d), 185(g)
& 185(j)

Nr. 185
(reverse)

Nr's. 185(a), 185(d), 185(g)
& 185(j) (Type B--for females)

186. **N.S.D.A.P. Long Service Awards**
    (Dienstauszeichnungen der N.S.D.A.P.)

(a)	Cross for 25 years, gilt and enamel	$900
(b)	Certificate	450
(c)	Case	150
(d)	Cross for 15 years, silver and enamel	150
(e)	Certificate	250
(f)	Carton	50
(g)	Cross for 10 years, bronze	100
(h)	Certificate	150
(i)	Carton	50

Nr. 186(a)

Nr. 185(d)

Nr. 186(d) (reverse)

Nr. 186(g)

Nr. 186(g) (reverse)

Nr. 187(a)

187. N.S.D.A.P. Golden Party Badge
(Goldenes Parteiabzeichen)

(a)	Type A	Official Adolf Hitler dated award "A.H." on reverse (30mm)	$750
(b)	Type B	25mm size (civilian dress) and 30mm size (N.S.D.A.P. uniform)	250-400
(c)		Certificate	350
(d)		Case, deluxe, for dual award of matched pair of badges	500

Nr's. 187(a) & 187(b) (30mm)

188. N.S.D.A.P. - "Blood Order" 1933
   (Blutorden)
(a) Type A First striking in hallmarked silver by
          Fuess München with buttonhole silk ribbon $1,000-1,500
(b)   Certificate .... 600+
(c)   Case, titled 300
(d) Type B Second striking in hallmarked silver without
          maker's mark and plain silk ribbon 600
(e)   Certificate 500
(f)   Large plain case 100

Nr's. 188(a) & 188(d)   Nr. 188(a)

J.R. Angolia

Nr. 188(e)

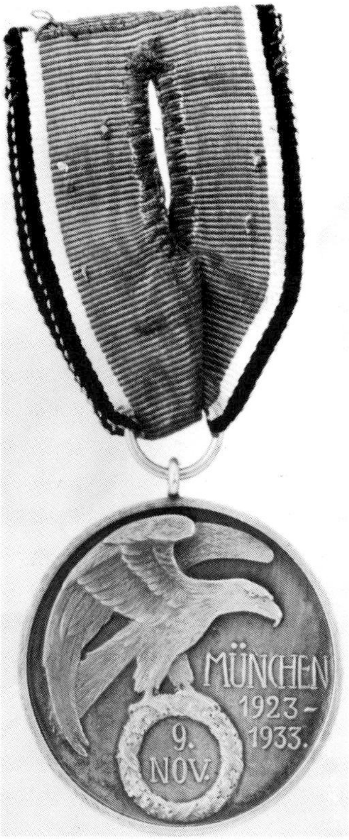
MÜNCHEN
1923-
1933.
9.
NOV.
Nr. 188(a)

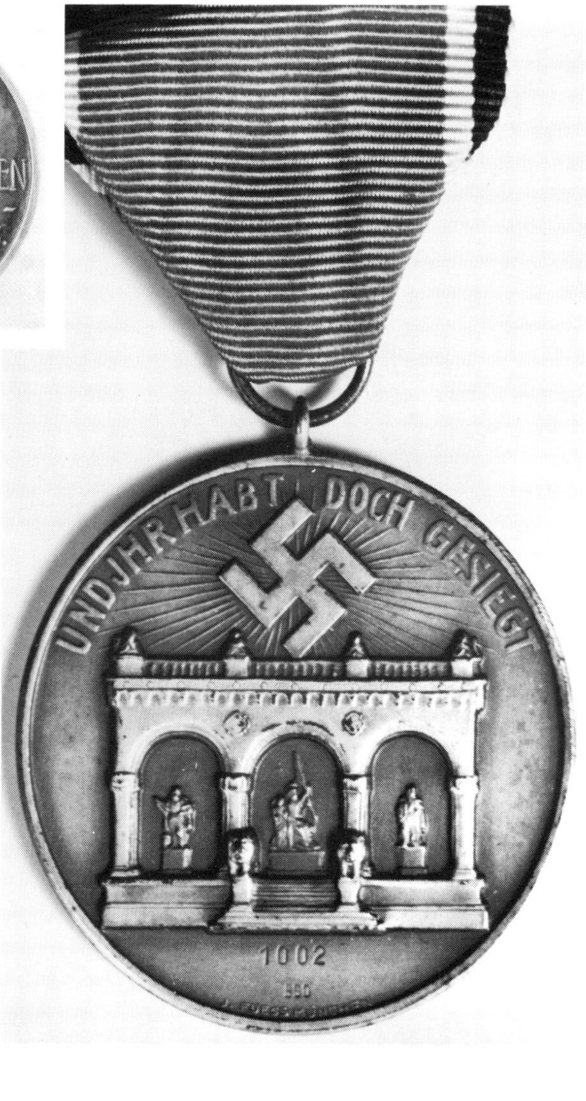
UND IHR HABT DOCH GESIEGT
1002
Nr. 188(a)
(reverse)

A. Southard

Heinrich Bennecke wears the Coburg Badge (Nr. 190).

J. Hanson

Heinrich Georg Graf Finck von Finckenstein wears the Nuremberg Badge of Honor (Nr. 191).

189. **Gau Munich Commemorative Badge 9 November 1923-33**
   (Gau München Erinnerungsabzeichen der 9.Nov.1923)
   Badge $100

Nr. 189

Nr. 190

190. **The Coburg Badge 1936**
   (Coburger Abzeichen)
(a) Type A Bronze $1,250
(b)   Certificate 250
(c)   Case 150
(d) Type B Unique example has been recorded in silver with
              red enamel swastika 2,000

191. **Nuremberg Badge of Honor 1929**
   (Nürnberger Parteitagsabzeichen 1929)
(a)   Variations exist in grey silver or gilt metal in
                solid and hollow back form $125-175
(b)   Certificate 125

Nr. 191

192. **Nuremberg Badge of Honor 1929 - Non-Portable Award**
   (Nürnberger Parteitagsabzeichen 1929)
(a)   Fine quality bronze, silver or gold-plated plaque
                in a deluxe leather titled case $250
(b)   Certificate 150

Nr. 192

Nr. 193
(Type A)

Bob Kraus

Nr. 193
(Type B)

193. **S.A. Ralley at Brunswick 1931 Badge of Honor**
   (Abzeichen des S.A. Treffens Braunschweig 1931)
   (a) Type A First pattern, large badge hollow back $150
   (b) Type B Variations exist in tin and aluminum 75
   (c) Certificate 75

194. **The "Frontbann" Badge 1924**
   (Frontbann-Abzeichen)
   Badge $400

Nr. 194

195. N.S.D.A.P. Party District Commemorative Badges 1933 (Traditions-Gau Abzeichen)

(a) Type A With either dates 1923 or 1925, fine quality hallmarked
silver with maker's stamp and black enamel $1,000
(b) Type B With either dates 1923 or 1925, fine quality hallmarked
silver with maker's stamp and black paint finish 750

Nr. 195   Nr. 195

196. Gau Berlin 1936

(a) Type A Fine quality gold plate & enamel with maker's
name and issue number $3,000
(b) Type B Fine quality silver plate & enamel with
maker's name and issue number 2,500
(c) Type C Late war manufacture in war metal and paint finish 1,000
(d)   Certificate 250
(e)   Case 150

Nr. 196

Nr. 197

197. Gau Baden 1933

(a) Type A Large oval gold-plated with maker's name $1,000
(b) Type B Large oval silver-plated with maker's name 800
(c) Type C Small round silver-plated badge.
Possibly for award to women 1,000
(d)   Certificate 200
(e)   Case 150

№ 000336 ✽

Besitz-Urkunde

zum Tragen des Ehren-
zeichens der Alten Garde
im Gau Hessen-Nassau
der Nationalsozialistischen
Deutschen Arbeiterpartei

Herrn *Kitzmann Heinz*
Ort *Frankfurt a. Main*
Straße *Wiesenhüttenstr. 16*
Mitgliedsnummer *45.562*
wird am heutigen Tage das Ehren-
zeichen 1925 der NSDAP, Gau
Hessen-Nassau, verliehen. Das
Recht zum Tragen des Zeichens er-
lischt mit dem Tage des Ausschei-
dens des Inhabers aus der Partei.

Frankfurt a. M.
den *6.7.34*

Nr. 195 certificate for "1925" commemorative badge.

**This NSKK-Brigadeführer wears
the Gau Baden Badge.**

198. Gau Thüringen 1936
   (Gauabzeichen für Thüringer)
(a)   Badge usually fine quality hallmarked silver although
          grey metal types exist $1,500
(b)   Certificate 250
(c)   Case 150

Nr. 198

199. East Hanover Gau Commemorative Badge 1933
   (Traditionsabzeichen des Gaues Osthannover der N.S.D.A.P.)
(a)   Gold Class $1,500
(b)   Certificate 250
(c)   Silver Class 1,000
(d)   Certificate 200
(e)   Bronze Class 500
(f)   Certificate 150

Nr. 199   Nr. 200

200. Gau Danzig Commemorative Badge 1939
   (Gau Traditionsabzeichen des Gaues Danzig Westpreussen)
(a)   Examples exist in hallmarked silver and in alloy $1,000-1,500
(b)   Certificate 500
201. Gau East Prussian Commemorative Badge 1938
   (Gau-Ehrenzeichen des Gaues Ostpreussen)
(a)   Variations exist in silver-plated metal with maker's
          stamp and white metal $1,000-1,500
(b)   Certificate 250

Nr. 201

202. **Gau Essen Commemorative Badge 1935**
(Gau-Traditionsabzeichen Essen)
Awarded in two classes, gilt and silvered alloy with maker's name, etc.

(a) Gilt Class $250
(b) Certificate 150
(c) Silver Class 200
(d) Certificate 100

Nr. 202

Nr. 203

203. **Gau Sudetenland Commemorative Badge 1938**
(Gau-Ehrenzeichen des Gaues Sudetenland der N.S.D.A.P.)

(a) Variations exist in both brass and deluxe hallmarked silver and enamel $1,000-2,000
(b) Certificate 250
(c) Case 150

173

This Political Leader at far right wears the Gau Sudetenland Commemorative Badge (Nr. 203).

This Labor Corps officer wears the dated Anhalt Labor Service Commemorative Badge (Nr. 206).

204. Gau Warthe Commemorative Badge 1939
(Gau Wartheland-Traditionsabzeichen)

(a)   Fine quality riveted, plated metal and enamel $3000

(b)   Miniature lapel pin, fine quality plated metal
and enamel pin back 750

(c)   Certificate 500

(d)   Case 200

Nr. 204

Nr. 205

205. H.J. Potsdam Badge 1932
(Potsdam-Abzeichen)

Bronze badge, pin back variations exist in silver
or grey metal $50-100

Nr. 206

206. Anhalt Labor Service Commemorative Badge 1932
(Anhalt Arbeitsdienst Erinnerungsabzeichen)

There are two versions of the badge, one bearing the
date 1932 and the other without a date.

(a)   Gilt Class $600

(b)   Silver Class 400

(c)   Steel Class - grey metal 300

207. Decoration of the Technical Emergency Service 1935
   (Ehrenzeichen der Technischen Nothilfe)
(a)   Awarded with the following dates: 1919, 1920, 1921, 1922, 1923 .... $400
(b)   Certificate 150
(c)   Case 50

Nr. 208

Nr. 207

208. "Stahlhelm" Commemorative Badges 1933
   (Traditions-Abzeichen des "Stahlhelm")
(a)   Awarded with the following dates: 1919, 1920, 1921, 1922, 1923
         1924, 1925, 1926, 1927, 1928, 1929, 1930, 1931, 1932
(b) Type A 34mm diameter $75
(c) Type B 30mm diameter 65

209. "Stahlhelm" Award Badges 1933

(a)   Bundestern, quality plated metal and enamel $750
(b)   Certificate 250
(c)   Wehrsportkreuz, quality plated metal and enamel 500
(d)   Certificate 150
(e)   Wehrsportabzeichen, white metal 75
(f)   Certificate 50

Nr. 209(c)

Nr. 209(a)

Nr. 209(e)

210. Danzig Cross 1939
(Danziger Kreuz)

(a)	1st Class Cross	$750
(b)	Certificate	350
(c)	Case	150
(d)	2nd Class Cross	450
(e)	Certificate	250
(f)	Case	100

Nr. 210(a)

Nr. 210(d)

211. Danzig Life Saving Medal
(Rettungsmedaille)

(a)	Medal	$900
(b)	Certificate	300

Nr. 211

Nr. 211
(reverse)

212. Danzig Fire Brigade Decoration 1939
(Feuerwehr-Ehrenzeichen)

(a)	1st Class Cross	$450
(b)	Certificate	150
(c)	2nd Class Cross	350
(d)	Certificate	150

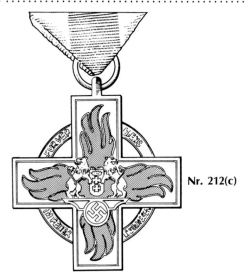

Nr. 212(c)

213. Danzig Faithful Service Decoration 1938
(Treudienst Ehrenzeichen)

(a)	Special Class Cross for 50 Years	$650
(b)	Certificate	450
(c)	1st Class Cross for 40 Years	550
(d)	Certificate	350
(e)	2nd Class Cross for 25 Years	450
(f)	Certificate	300

Nr. 213

**Der Präsident
des Senats der Freien Stadt Danzig**

Als Anerkennung für **25** jährige treue Dienste
für Volk und Staat verleihe ich

dem Schmied

Paul Groth
—

das

Treudienst-Ehrenzeichen
der Freien Stadt Danzig
in Silber

Danzig, den 9. November 1938

Nr. 213(f)

Nr's. 214(a) & 214(c)

**214. Danzig Police Long Service Awards 1938
(Polizei-Dienstauszeichnungen)**

(a)	1st Class Cross for 25 Years	$650
(b)	Certificate	450
(c)	2nd Class Cross for 18 Years	500
(d)	Certificate	350
(e)	Silver Medal for 8 Years	400
(f)	Certificate	300

Nr. 214(e)   Nr. 214(e) (reverse)

215. Danzig Red Cross Decorations
       (Ehrenzeichen des Roten Kreuzes)

(a)   Decoration of Merit $650
(b)   Certificate 400
(c)   Cross of Merit 1st Class for 25 Years 550
(d)   Certificate 300
(e)   Cross of Merit 2nd Class for 10 Years 400
(f)   Certificate 250

Nr. 215(c)

Nr. 215(a)

Nr. 215(e)

216. Danzig Flak Battle Badge of the City
(Flakkampfabzeichen der Stadt Danzig)
(a)   Fine quality silver striking $1,500
(b)   Certificate 500

Nr. 216

217. N.S.F.K. Badge for Powered Aircraft Pilot (1st Design) 1938
(Abzeichen für Motorflugzeugführer)
(a)   Fine quality silver bullion on cloth backing
         in patch form $1,250
(b)   Certificate 750
(c)   (2nd Design) 1942. Struck in silver-plated brass,
         numbered on reverse 1,800
(d)   Certificate 750
(e)   Case 300

George Petersen

Nr. 217(a)

Nr. 217(c)

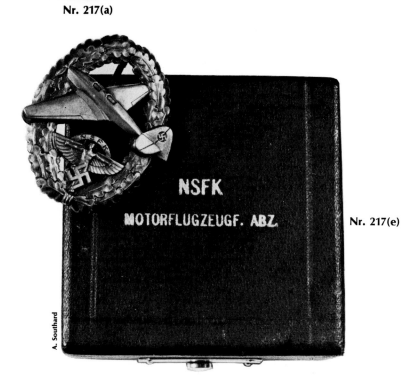

NSFK

MOTORFLUGZEUGF. ABZ.

A. Southard

Nr. 217(e)

218. N.S.F.K. Badge for Powered Aircraft Pilot (3rd Design) 1943 (Abzeichen für Motorflugzeugführer)

(a)	Struck in grey metal, numbered on reverse	$2,000
(b)	Certificate	750
(c)	Case	300

Nr. 218

219. N.S.F.K. Badge for Free Balloon Pilot (1st Design) 1938
(Abzeichen für Freiballonführer)

(a)   Fine quality silver bullion on cloth backing in patch form $750

(b)   Certificate 750

Nr. 219

Nr. 220

220. N.S.F.K. Badge for Free Balloon Pilot (2nd Design) c. 1943
(Abzeichen für Freiballonführer)

(a)   Silver grey metal, numbered on reverse $2,000

(b)   Certificate 750

(c)   Case 300   **183**

221. N.S.F.K. Large Glider Pilot's Badge 1942
(Grosses Segelflieger-Abzeichen)

(a)	Badge	$1,200
(b)	Certificate	900
(c)	Case	250

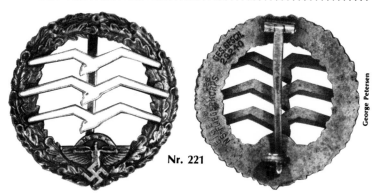

Nr. 221

George Petersen

222. N.S.F.K. Aero-Modeling Proficiency Badges
(N.S.F.K. Modell-Flugleistungsabzeichen)

(a)	Grade A round badge.....................................	$500
(b)	Certificate	300
(c)	Grade B round badge.....................................	400
(d)	Certificate	250
(e)	Grade C round badge	300
(f)	Certificate	200

Nr. 222(a) (white thread)

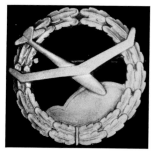

Nr. 222(e)

223. S.A. Military Sports Badge
(S.A. Wehrabzeichen)

(a)	1st Class in Gold	$125
(b)	Certificate	75
(c)	2nd Class in Silver	85
(d)	Certificate	50
(e)	3rd Class in Bronze	25
(f)	Certificate	25

J.R. Angolia

Nr. 223(f)

224. **S.A. Military Sports Badge for War Wounded 1943**
     (S.A. Wehrabzeichen für Kriegsversehrte)
(a)   Badge $250
(b)   Certificate 125

Nr. 224

Document authorizing the recipient to wear the D.R.A. Sports Badge in Gold (Nr. 225(b)).

(Left and above) The D.R.A. Sports Badge (Nr. 225) in wear.

(Left and below) The D.R.L. Sports Badge (Nr. 227) in wear.

225. D.R.A. Sports Badges c. 1933
   (Deutsches Reichsabzeichen für Leibesübungen)
   First design without Swastika

(a)   1st Class in Gold $80
(b)   Certificate 40
(c)   2nd Class in Silver 40
(d)   Certificate 30
(e)   3rd Class in Bronze 20
(f)   Certificate 20

Nr. 225   Nr. 226

226. D.R.L. Sports Badges pre-1937
   (Deutsches Reichsabzeichen für Leibesübungen)
   Second design without Swastika

(a)   1st Class in Gold $80
(b)   Certificate 50-60
(c)   2nd Class in Silver 40
(c)   2nd Class in Silver 40
(d)   Certificate 40-45
(e)   3rd Class in Bronze 20
(f)   Certificate 35-40

227. D.R.L. Sports Badge 1937
   (Deutsches Reichsabzeichen für Leibesübungen)
   Third design with Swastika

(a)   1st Class in Gold $125
(b)   Certificate 60

Nr's. 227 & 228

228. **D.R.L. Sports Badge for War Disabled 1942**
(Versehrtensport-Abzeichen)
(a) Badge (Silver with gold wreath) $150
(b) Certificate 125

George Petersen

... Prüfungen der **Gruppe 5** bestanden, indem $\frac{er}{sie}$

(Name des Bewerbers
der Bewerberin)
(Von einem der Prüfer eigenhändig mit Tinte auszufüllen)

10000 m in 45 Min 34²/10 Meh gelaufen ist

Dienstsiegel
der zuständigen
Behörde, der
Unterstufe oder
des die Prüfung
abnehmenden
Truppenteils

Eigenhändige Unterschrift des Bewerbers
(Vor- und Zuname): der Bewerberin

Ort:

Datum 24. 2. .... 19 44

Unterschrift des Obmanns

Eigenhändige Unterschrift der beiden gleichzeitig anwesenden Prüfer:

1.   2.   Hauptfeldwebel

Nummer des Prüferausweises   Nummer des Prüferausweises

Nr.

wird hiermit, nachdem die Bedingungen erfüllt find, das

Reichssportabzeichen

verliehen.

, den 2. März 1944.

Stellvertreter des Reichssportführers.

Berliner Buchdruckerel Union, GmbH., Berlin C 2, Dircksenstr. 41, Tel. 41 81 81

Nr. 227(b)

229. Achievement and Championship Badges of the N.S.R.L. and D.R.L.
(Leistungsabzeichen und Meisterschaftsabzeichen des N.S.R.L. und D.R.L.)
    Lapel badges

(a)   Achievement badge in bronze with date $75
(b)   Certificate 35
(c)   Achievement badge in bronze without date 50
(d)   Certificate 20
(e)   Achievement badge in silver with date 150
(f)   Certificate 45
(g)   Achievement badge in silver without date 100
(h)   Certificate 40
(i)   Championship badge in gold 175
(j)   Certificate 50

Nr. 229(a)   Nr. 229(c)

230. S.A. German Expert Horseman's Badge 1937
(Deutsche Reiterführer-Abzeichen)

(a)   Fine quality silver badge with maker's stamp
    and issue number $2,000
(b)   Certificate 750

Nr. 230

231. German Horseman's Sports Badge
(Deutsches Reiterabzeichen)
(a)   1st Class in Gold $125
(b)   Certificate 75
(c)   2nd Class in Silver 75
(d)   Certificate 45
(e)   3rd Class in Bronze 50
(f)   Certificate 35

Nr. 231

Nr. 232

Nr. 233

232. German Horse Driver's Badge
(Deutsches Fahrer-Abzeichen)
(a)   1st Class in Gold $150
(b)   Certificate 75
(c)   2nd Class in Silver 100
(d)   Certificate 45
(e)   3rd Class in Bronze 60
(f)   Certificate 35

233. Badge for the Care of Horses 1937
(Deutsche Pferdepflegerabzeichen)
(a)   Grade I in Gold $175
(b)   Certificate 65
(c)   Grade II in Silver 125
(d)   Certificate 45
(e)   Grade III in Bronze 100
(f)   Certificate 30

234. German Young Horseman's Sports Badge
(Deutsches Jugend-Reiterabzeichen)
(a)   Badge $80
(b)   Certificate 100

Nr. 234

235. N.S.R.K. Plaque for Donations of Horses 1937
(Plakette für Zurverfügungstellung von Pferdern, u.s.w.)
(a)   Plaque $100
(b)   Document 50
(c)   Case 30

Nr. 235

Nr. 235
(reverse)

236. 236 German Motor Sports Badge 1939
(Deutsches Motorsportabzeichen)
(a)   1st Class in Gold $2,500
(b)   Certificate 500
(c)   2nd Class in Silver 2,000
(d)   Certificate 350
(e)   3rd Class in Bronze 1,500
(f)   Certificate 300
(g)   Case 200

Nr. 236

**237. Germanic Proficiency Runes Sport Badge 1943
(Germanische Leistungsrune)**
        Bronzed or silver-washed (matt) on grey war metal
        and on reverse prongs to attach Sigrunes
(a)   Silver Grade Badge $1,250
(b)   Certificate 750
(c)   Bronze Grade Badge 1,000
(d)   Certificate 750

Nr. 237

Himmler makes the first
presentation of the above
badge to the Dutch SS in
Holland, in February 1944.

238. National Sports Leader's Medallion "For an Outstanding Achievement" 1933
(Reichssportfuhrer Medaille "Im Anerkennung Einer Hervorragenden Leistung")
(a)   Medallion $150
(b)   Certificate 150

Nr. 238   Nr. 238 (reverse)

239. National Youth Sports Badge
(Reichsjugend Sportabzeichen)
(a)   R.J.A. silver lapel badge $20
(b)   Certificate 20

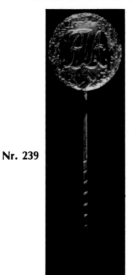

Nr. 239

Nr. 240

240. H.J. Golden Leader's Sports Badge 1937
(Goldenes Führer-Sportabzeichen)
(a)   Badge $250
(b)   Certificate 150

This Hitler Youth leader wears the Golden Leader's Sports Badge.

241. German Youth Champion's Badge of Honor 1942
      (Ehrennadel des Deutschen Jugendmeisters)
(a)   "Jugendmeister" Badge in Gold $1,500
(b)   Certificate 600
(c)   "Kampfspiele" Badge in Silver 350
(d)   Certificate 450
(e)   "Kampfspiele" Badge in Bronze 250
(f)   Certificate 250

Nr. 241   Nr. 242

242. National Champion's Badge of Honor 1942
      (Ehrennadel der Reichssieger)
(a)   1st Class in Gold $550
(b)   Certificate 400
(c)   2nd Class in Silver 350
(d)   Certificate 350
(e)   3rd Class in Bronze 300
(f)   Certificate 200

243. Hitler Youth Proficiency Badge 1934
      (Leistungsabzeichen der Hitler Jugend)
(a)   Grade I in Silver, white metal $30
(b)   Certificate 25
(c)   Grade II in Bronze 40
(d)   Certificate 25
(e)   Grade III in Black 45
(f)   Certificate 25

Nr. 243(e)

Nr. 243(a)

Hasher

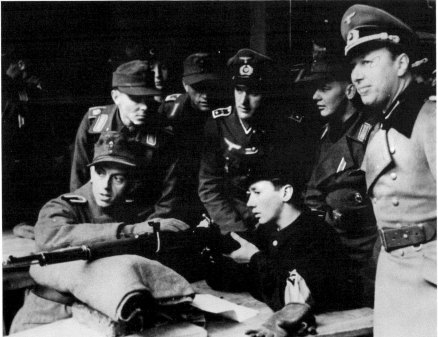

Oberst Niemack and members of Panzer-Grenadier-Division "Grossdeutschland" visit a Hitler Youth shooting range where youngsters are attempting to qualify.

244. **Hitler Youth Expert Skier Badge c.1934**
   (H.J. Skiführerabzeichen)
   (a)   Badge $2,500
   (b)   Certificate 750

Nr. 244

245. **German Young People's Shooting Award**
   (Schiessauszeichning des Deutschen Jungvolks)
   (a)   D.J. Shooting Badge $30
   (b)   Certificate 20

Nr. 245

246. **Hitler Youth Shooting Awards**
   (Hitler Jugend Schiessauszeichnungen)
   (a)   Badge for Good Shots $50
   (b)   Certificate 25
   (c)   Badge for Marksmanship (Silver) 100
   (d)   Certificate 40
   (e)   Badge for Champion Shots (Gold) 250
   (f)   Certificate 60

Nr. 246(a)     Nr. 246(e)

247. **German Young People's Proficiency Badge**
   (Leistungsabzeichen des Deutschen Jungvolks)
   (a)   Silver Grade Badge - white metal $30
   (b)   Certificate 20
   (c)   Iron Grade Badge - blackened metal 35
198 (d)   Certificate 20

Nr. 247

248. League of German Girls' Proficiency Clasp
(B.D.M. Leistungsabzeichen)
(a)   Silver Grade Clasp $200
(b)   Certificate 80
(c)   Bronze Grade Clasp 125
(d)   Certificate 50

Nr. 248

249. Young Girls' Proficiency Clasp
(Jungmädel Leistungsabzeichen)
(a)   Silver Clasp $150
(b)   Certificate 80

Nr. 249

250. Victor's Badge in the National Trade Competition (H.J.) 1938
(Siegerabzeichen im Reichsberufswettkampf)
(a)   Kreissieger Badge with date: 1938, 1939, 1940, 1941, 1942, 1943, 1944 . $150
(b)   Certificates 150
(c)   Gausieger Badge with date: 1938, 1939, 1940, 1941, 1942, 1943, 1944 .. 250
(d)   Certificates 180
(e)   Reichssieger Badge with date: 1928, 1939, 1940, 1941, 1942, 1943, 1944 500
(f)   Certificates 300
        Badges with the last date "1944" are usually grey war
        metal with painted details rather than enamel. A cruder
        badge, but rare.

Nr. 250(a)

Nr. 250(c)

Nr. 250(e)

Nr. 250(b)

251. **Decoration of the National Socialist German Students Federation**
(Ehrenzeichen des N.S.D. Studentenbundes)
Decoration $150

Nr. 251

252. Golden Hitler Youth Badge of Honor with Oak Leaves 1935
   (Goldenes H.J. Ehrenzeichen mit Eichenlaub)
(a)   Early awards in hallmarked gold and enamel; later
             awards fine quality hallmarked silver-gilt and enamel $900-1,500
(b)   Certificates 750

Nr. 252

Reichsleiter Rosenberg wear-
ing the Golden Hitler Youth
Badge of Honor and the
Golden Party Badge.

Nr. 253

253. Golden Hitler Youth Badge of Honor 1934
   (Goldenes Hitler Jugend Ehrenabzeichen)
(a)   Badge $125
(b)   Certificate 150

254. Decoration of the High Command of the Hitler Youth for
   Distinguished Foreigners 1941
   (Ehrenzeichen der Reichsjugendführung der H.J. for
   Verdiente Ausländer)
(a)   Decoration $550
(b)   Certificate 300

Nr. 254

255. **Medallion "For the Furthering of Hitler Youth Hostel Building Program" 1937**
(Plakette "Für die Förderung der Heimbeschaffung der H.J.")
Medallion $300

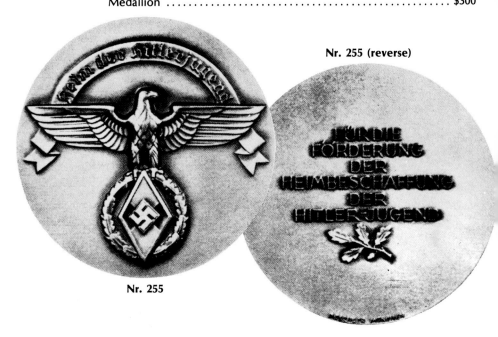

Nr. 255 (reverse)

Nr. 255

256. **Civil Pilot's Badge c.1936**
(Civil Flugzeugführer)
(a) Badge $600
(b) Certificate 450
(c) Case 200

Nr. 256(a)

Nr. 256(c)

Verleihungsurkunde

Ich verleihe dem

Flugzeugführer

Herbert S c h r a m m

das Zivil-Abzeichen für

Flugzeugführer

Münster i. W., den 20. September 1936

Der Befehlshaber im Luftkreis IV

Halm

General der Flieger.

Nr. 10/36

NSFK-Obertruppführer Peter Habicht, gliding instructor from NSFK-Standarte 81 (Neustadt), wears the Civil Pilot's Badge.

257. **Civil Radio Operator's Badge**
     (Civil Bordfunker)
(a)   Badge $400
(b)   Certificate 400
(c)   Case 200

Nr. 257(a)

George Petersen

Bordfunkerabzeichen

Nr. 257(c)

258. Civil Gliding Proficiency Badge
(Segelflieger-Abzeichen)

(a)	"A" Certificate (one gull) Badge	$20-40
(b)	Certificate	50
(c)	"B" Certificate Badge (two gulls)	30-40
(d)	Certificate	60
(e)	"C" Certificate Badge (three gulls)	40-60
(f)	Certificate	60
(g)	Achievement "C" Certificate Badge (three gulls within oakleaf wreath)	150
(h)	Certificate	80

Nr. 258(e) Nr. 258(g)

259. German Female Railway Staff Service Badge 1944
(Dienstnadel für Eisenbahnerinnen)

(a)	Gold Class (Not awarded)	*
(b)	Silver Class	$350
(c)	Bronze Class	250

Nr. 259

THIRD REICH MEDAL RELATED REFERENCE BOOKS
OLD & NEW
(Brief review only)

1. "ORDEN UND EHRENZEICHEN IM DRITTEN REICH"
   By Dr. H. DOEHLE (Berlin, 1939 & 1943 Editions)
   Hardback in black & white, also deluxe colour editions.

2. "UNIFORMEN-MARKT"
   Official Third Reich monthly publications, usually found bound by year.
   Issued for years 1935, 36, 37, 38, 39, 40, 41, 42, 43 & 44, plus a few issues in 1945. Superb reference works, included illustrations of newly instituted awards, daggers, new regulations, uniforms, patches and insignia, both German and foreign volunteers, etc.

3. "DEUTSCHE AUSZEICHNUNGEN" (BAND I & II)
   By Dr. KURT G. KLIETMANN (Berlin, Band I-1957 and Band II-1971) - GERMAN AWARDS & BADGES 1871-1945.

   BAND I (1957) - German text. All medals and awards with code-ref numbers and superb photographs (ribbon chart).

   BAND II (1971) - German text. Superbly laid out study of medals and awards, dealt with in a scientific manner and easy to understand, even for non-German language readers.

   This monumental work was the first serious study of awards, also from a historic point of view, and still remains the BIBLE on the subject! All serious historians, authors and students of the subject agree on this. This is shown by the large number of publications dedicated to his name and by the large number of photographs credited in modern books to his Berlin Institute, both in English and German language editions. Perhaps one day an English translation or edition will be available so that all collectors everywhere will have access to this superb reference work.

   Awards are not only cod-ref numbered but details are also given on types of material or metals used, exact sizes and weights, types of manufacture, how and where worn, ribbons. etc. Also listed are known copies or fakes and finally for each and every item there is a long list of sources - such as other books used, letters, discussion with manufacturers, names of recipients and Third Reich ref-sources (official, military and political), articles, journals, etc.

4. "ORDERS, DECORATIONS, MEDALS & BADGES OF THE THIRD REICH" (VOL. I)
   By DAVID LITTLEJOHN & COL. C.M. DODKINS, CBE (Bender Books, USA, 1968)

   First real reference work in English language. Many good illustrations and good basic text. Possibly more widely known in the United States and Great Britain than any other work on the subject.

5. "ORDERS, DECORATIONS, MEDALS & BADGES OF THE THIRD REICH" (VOL. II)
By DAVID LITTLEJOHN & COL. C.M. DODKINS, CBE (Bender Books, USA, 1973)
Second in this series, dealing with Nazi puppet states, etc. Also, corrections and extra information to VOL. I (1968). An excellent work.

6. "FOR FÜHRER AND FATHERLAND" (MILITARY AWARDS - VOL. I)
By LTC J. ANGOLIA (Bender Books, USA, 1976)
Another Bender book, by an author previously known for his interest in Nazi edged weapons, daggers, etc. A much thicker book, with many photographs of awards and citations. List of all sources at back of book. Added to previous books on this list should cover almost all the items of which collectors should be aware!

7. "FOR FÜHRER AND FATHERLAND" (POLITICAL AWARDS - VOL. II)
By LTC J. ANGOLIA (Bender Books, USA, 1978)
As Volume I but covering political awards, plus an addendum to VOL. I.

8. "THE PRUSSIAN & GERMAN IRON CROSS"
By V.E. BOWEN (England, Private Publication - 1986) (1000 copies only)
Although dealing only with the Iron Cross, this superb work is highly recommended to any serious collector or dealer. Following in the tradition of Dr. Klietmann's books, with a truly scientific approach. Well laid out, with much historical information. Many actual Third Reich awards are illustrated, with sizes, weights, etc. Also, much information regarding copies, etc. Many sources quoted. In fact, THE work on the subject in the English language.

9. "THE IRON CROSS OF PRUSSIA & GERMANY"
By A.E. PROWSE (New Zealand, Private Publication - 1971)
First work of its kind in the English Language and until Heyde's book (German text) and lately Bowen's book this was the BIBLE in the English language. An excellent work, well laid out and listing all sources. Much historical award data on 1939-45 awards.

10. "THE IRON CROSS 1813-1870-1914"
By F. HEYDE (German text - 1980)
Excellent photographs. Again a very professional and scientific approach and easy for non-German language readers to understand. Recommended by Mr. Bowen in his own monumental work. (Does not cover 1939-45 period.)

11. "THE POUR LE MÉRITE"
By Dr. KURT G. KLIETMANN (Berlin, 1966)
Many excellent photographs. Misleading title. Book covers in a

scientific and historical manner the awards of Imperial Germany and her allies, also Third Reich 1939-45 and Axis powers, etc. An excellent reference work, even after twenty years!

12. "AUSZEICHNUNGEN DES DEUTSCHEN REICHES, 1936-1945"
By Dr. KURT G. KLIETMANN (Berlin, 1981)
Many references to documentation on civil and military awards, etc. 240 pages. Over 250 illustrations and photographs, including many rare items, some not seen in books before. Also, details and illustrations on award documents and recipients, plus manufacturer's variations and fakes.

13. "COMBAT MEDALS OF THE THIRD REICH"
By C.J. AILSBY (P. Stephens - 1987)
A new British work, written by a collector. Mr. Ailsby has failed to list the complete sources for his statements, figures and facts. In the light of this omission the work cannot be recommended to the serious historian or student of the subject. The mere mention of the Bender Publications by Littlejohn and Dodkins and by LTC Angolia, with vague references to correspondence, are not enough to substantiate in-depth historical or factual information.

This last work has received very bad press release-news from experts on the subject, such as Dr. Klietmann & German INFO (Issue 54 Jan. 1988) of the German Orders & Medals Collectors' Society. Many illustrations of known copies & fakes, which new collectors or dealers will assume to be original pre-1945. Fortunately, experienced collectors & honest dealers will know better!